Veneer Technologies, Inc.
Lean Six-Sigma Yellow Belt (LSSY)

Lean Six-Sigma Yellow Belt

Best Practices for Operational Excellence

Veneer Technologies, Inc.

Merwan Mehta, Ph.D.
(MehtaM@ECU.edu)
Professor
College of Engineering & Technology
EAST CAROLINA UNIVERSITY

Instructor: Merwan Mehta, Ph.D.

- Professor; Technology Systems; College of Engineering and Technology; since 2004
- Consulting in Operational Excellence since 2000
  - Various companies in U.S., Canada, Mexico, and India, U.S. DOD, Thermo Fisher, Dyneema, Spirit Aerosystems, ASMO, ECU, ECU-Health, Halifax Hospital, Bosch, Hitachi, Vidant-Health Chowan Edenton, Bosch, etc.
- Coordinator for B.S. in Industrial Engineering Technology program at ECU
- Coordinator for Lean Six-Sigma Black Belt Certificate program at ECU
- Technical Partner in 2 businesses; operations, product design, technology
- Sr. Project Director; Manufacturing Extension Partnership, Rolla, Missouri
- Ph.D. in Engineering Management, Lean Six-Sigma Black Belt Trainer (Institute of Industrial and Systems Engineers)

College of Engineering & Technology
EAST CAROLINA UNIVERSITY

Veneer Technologies, Inc.
Lean Six-Sigma Yellow Belt (LSSYB) Training

Discussion Topics – Day 1

- Case study in culture change using operational excellence principles
- Introduction to basic operational principles of LSS
- Experiences of leading companies like Toyota in reducing waste
- Building consensus & using self-reflection for decision making and mistake handling
- Creating a customer centered organization focused on waste reduction and profitability
- The DMAIC Process for improving processes for waste reduction and efficiency
- Conquering complexity in processes to increase efficiency
- Team ideas to create a high performing organization
- Civility and self-improvement
- Creating a simulated process to gather data to analyze waste and rework in processes

Discussion Topics – Day 2

- Lean thinking, value stream and eight classical wastes found in all organizations
- The effect of batch and continuous flow of outputs in processes
- Use of Kanban and Takt time to satisfy customer requirements
- Process balancing & activity efficiency (AE) to eliminate waste in processes
- Use of Histograms to track cycle time for processes to control waste through variation
- Case study in waste reduction and efficiency improvement: 3C Store Fixtures Inc., NC
- Using first pass yield and rolled throughput yield to control waste of defects and rework
- Using the metric of defects per million opportunities (DPMO) to control defects
- Use of basic quality tools of 5-Why analysis and the 7 tools of quality

College of Engineering & Technology
EAST CAROLINA UNIVERSITY

Veneer Technologies, Inc.
Lean Six-Sigma Yellow Belt (LSSYB) Training

Culture Change Case Study

- MANUFACTURING INSIGHTS: Building a Lean Culture: Turnaround efforts at the H. I. D. Global Company*
  * Copyright © 2006 Society of Manufacturing Engineers (DVD available on SME.org)

- Manufacturer of contactless control cards and readers for the security industry
- Ninety-six employees; on the brink of closing its doors forever

- On Youtube accepting the Connecticut Shingo Prize:
- https://www.youtube.com/watch?v=7ISdvdxXWog

Lean Culture - DVD

Highlights from Case Study

- Lead time was 25 days and operation time was 14 to 22 seconds
- Holistic approach: the goal was to break down barriers
- Soft stuff is the hard stuff! Morale improvement team was formed!
- Belief was that you cannot have quality and on-time delivery
- Misery index = # of late products in a line times # of days late
- Example: 20 late orders by 5 days and 10 late by 10 days
- Misery index = (20 x 5) + (10 x 10) = 200
- Instituted a group incentive program with five ways to achieve points
- Proactive approach to hiring people; positive attitude: no CAVE mentality
- CAVE = Citizens against virtually everything

College of Engineering & Technology
EAST CAROLINA UNIVERSITY

Veneer Technologies, Inc.
Lean Six-Sigma Yellow Belt (LSSYB) Training

Highlights from Case Study

- We can get caught up in day-to-day tasks and fire-fighting
- It is easy for us to accept status-quo as normal. Normalization of deviance
- Management should constantly keep promoting efficiency ideas
  - Safety, teamwork, standard procedure
  - Provider metrics to know how well things are going!
  - Encourage making things a little better everyday!
  - Continuously challenge employees to be mindful (be in the present)
  - Promote empowerment of employees
  - Provide employees positive examples and role models to succeed
- Make it all visual; make it ugly—let all bad things stare in your face!
- Transfer ownership of quality to operators

Compass for Achieving Annual Goals

- Employees produced their own goals and created a compass for the year
- 20 employees created 4 points of the compass
- Only 4 most important goals were selected

- Improved delivery speed
- Improved quality: 10,000 / 1,500 E DPMO
- Improved delivery: 98/95
- Innovation: 2 ideas implemented per person per month

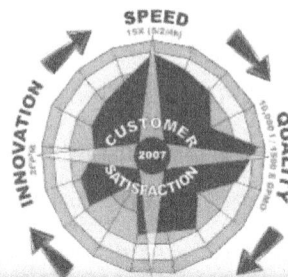

College of Engineering & Technology
EAST CAROLINA UNIVERSITY

Comments from Employees

- Facilities Manager, Security & Safety Coordinator; September 14, 2015
- Great place to work and develop new skills
- Enjoyed opportunities to advance skills and working with talented people
- Lead facilities person; July 15, 2015
- Great lean culture
- Like family….we all got along well
- Hardest part was leaving at the end of the day!

- Great company to work for. Enabled me to grow in my responsibilities
- Management was good at promoting people from within
- Lots of teamwork
- People move up from production floor to management positions
- HID is relocating to Texas. If not for the relocation I would not be searching for a new position

Employee reviews on Indeed.com for HID Global, Inc. Retrieved April 3rd, 2017.

Overview of Lean Principles

- Elimination of all wasted resources to increase productivity & profitability
- Holistic thinking
  - All business processes
- Openness and flexibility; transparency and fairness
- Burning platform
- Motivation - WIIFM (what's in it for me?)

- "The Machine That Changed The World"
- 90 plants in 17 countries

- The Toyota Production System (TPS)

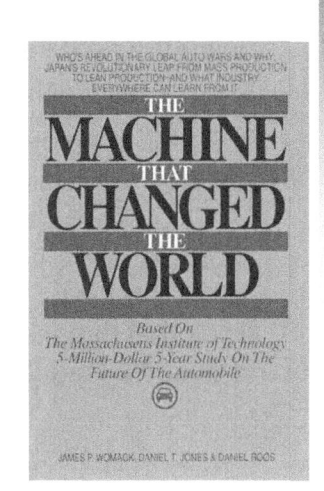

Veneer Technologies, Inc.
Lean Six-Sigma Yellow Belt (LSSYB) Training

Comparing Auto Plants in the World

Company	Japanese	Japanese	American	European
Location	Japan	America	America	Europe
Hours/vehicle	16.8	21.2	25.1	36.2
Defects/100	60	65	82.3	97
Sq ft/vehicle	5.7	9.1	7.8	7.8
Repair to assembly area	4.10%	4.90%	12.90%	14.40%
Inventory (days for 8 parts)	0.2	1.6	2.9	2
% workforce in teams	69%	71%	17%	0.60%
Job rotations (0 to 4)	3	2.7	0.9	1.9
Suggestions/employee	61.6	1.4	0.4	0.4
Job classes	11.9	8.7	67.1	14.8
New worker training hours	380	370	46	173
Absenteeism	5	4.8	11.7	12.1
Automation in welding	86%	85%	76%	76%
Automation in painting	54%	41%	34%	38%
Automation in assembly	1.70%	1.10%	1.20%	3.10%

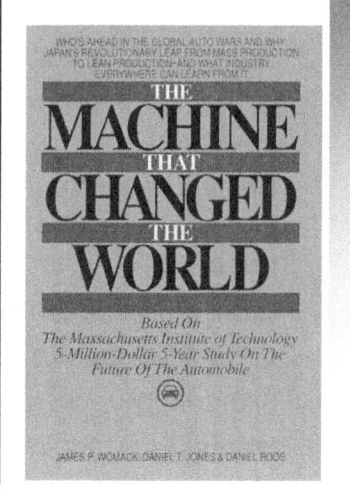

IMVP World Assembly Plant Survey (1989)

TOYOTA MOTOR COMPANY

- Major contribution: real-life example of a modern corporation thriving in a capitalistic world, while doing the right thing
- Short-term profits are not the first goal
- 359,542* employees (2020 with COVID); is run like a family business
    - Employees have a sense of purpose
    - Do the right thing for customers, employees, and society
- Book that Japanese managers credit for ideas of total quality practices

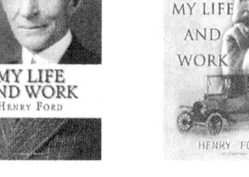

*https://www.statista.com/statistics/294192/number-of-toyota-employees/

College of Engineering & Technology
EAST CAROLINA UNIVERSITY

The Toyota Production System (TPS)

- Design out complexity (muri), control inconsistency (mura) and eliminate waste (muda)
- Muda: TIM WOOD
- Gains in productivity and quality come from unified management and employees with a commitment to positive change
  - Just-in-time: making only what is needed, when it is needed and, in the amount, it is needed
  - Jidoka: Autonomation; automation with a human touch

Consensus …..

- A search for the best decision
- Come to one solution through everyone's best thinking
- May not be everyone's first choice
- Everyone may not be completely satisfied
- All understand why decision is the best one to pursue
- Everyone has a chance to put forth their ideas and opinions
- Allow interaction between team members to understand where each comes from
- No silent disagreements
- Everyone buys in the idea of what consensus is and is not

The Toyota Way – Decision Making

- Careful upfront planning leads to flawless implementation
- Consider everything, to do right the first time
- Implement decisions rapidly
- How decisions are made is as important as quality of decisions
- Wrong decisions are okay if right process was used
- Core Lesson:
  - Develop a system, stick with it and improve it!
  - Philosophy, learning and innovation starts from the top
  - Believe in long-term thinking and continuity of leadership
  - Work to create industrious, humble, and a learning culture

Toyota - Culture Change Ideas

- Start from the top—shakeup executive leadership if needed
- Involve from the bottom up
- Use middle managers as change agents
- Understand that it takes time to develop people who understand and live the philosophy
- Understand it is extremely difficult to create right culture

Veneer Technologies, Inc.
Lean Six-Sigma Yellow Belt (LSSYB) Training

The Process of Lean

- Define value; what do you provide and how?
  - What does the customer want?
- Understand and document flow of value
  - Where is value created and how?
- Identify non-value-added tasks & eliminate
  - All work is value-enhancing or waste
- Standardize processes:
  - Eliminate complexity
  - Focus on lead time and pull
- Strive for perfection
  - Keep doing – continuous improvement

Birth of Six-Sigma

- Bill Smith, engineer & CEO Bob Galvin
  - Defects per thousand is not good enough
  - Defects per million opportunities (DPMO)
  - Six-sigma process: 3.4 defects/million
  - New standard, methodology and cultural change
  - Documented > $16B in savings
  - Could have saved $5B in 4 years in service functions at Motorola

- 1st iteration at Motorola: Defect reduction
- 2nd iteration at General Electric: Cost reduction
- 3rd iteration everywhere: Value creation

College of Engineering & Technology
EAST CAROLINA UNIVERSITY

Veneer Technologies, Inc.
Lean Six-Sigma Yellow Belt (LSSYB) Training

Operational Excellence Implementation

- Wide variety of ideas & DMAIC process

> Define → Measure → Analyze → Improve → Control

- Needs a strong and constant thrust from management
- Top management should articulate the need for change
- Provide reasoning as to what might happen if change is not successfully implemented
- Needs a burning desire in the heart of top managers
  - Burning platform
  - What's in it for me (WIIFM)

The DMAIC Process

- Let team know what is expected
- Champion and process improvement team are fully involved

> Define → Measure → Analyze → Improve → Control

- Champion owns the projects and improvement initiatives
- Toll gate review: formal review of each phase
- Project not allowed to proceed
- Complete each gate before moving forward
- No backtracking to a previous stage

College of Engineering & Technology
EAST CAROLINA UNIVERSITY

Veneer Technologies, Inc.
Lean Six-Sigma Yellow Belt (LSSYB) Training

Reduce Complexity

- The payoff from reducing complexity dwarf's process improvement returns
- Introduce only value-added complexity
  - Additional requirements for satisfying different customers
- Non-value-added complexity
  - Evolved complexity and unexamined complexity
- Mitsubishi Machine Tools
  - Only six fasteners
- International Power Machines (IPM)
  - Uninterruptible Power Supplies from 5 kw to 300 kw
  - No common parts; 6-12 weeks delivery
  - After complexity reduction
    - Gross profit from 18% to 37%
    - Operating profit from -3% to 20%

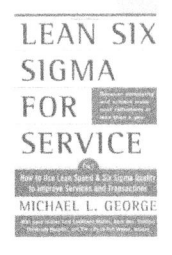

American Airlines Case Study

- Unacceptable on-time departure (CTQ)
- Culprit: too much of a differentiated service offering
  - 30 sub-fleets; 14 different airplanes; 757 aircrafts w/ & w/o life rafts
  - Small planes with too many 1st class seats
- Opposite strategy pursued by Southwest Airlines
- President of AA, Mr. Gerard Arpey:
  - Cost of complexity isn't offset by what you can charge
  - Complexity creates opportunities for you to fail your customer
- Strategy:
  - Reduced aircrafts; 14 to 7; Mechanics closer; better process flow
- Results in 18 months
  - On-time performance from 5th to 2nd; customer complaints down by ½

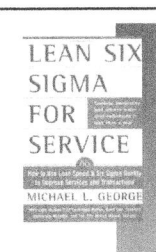

College of Engineering & Technology
EAST CAROLINA UNIVERSITY

Empower Employees

- Senior managers spend a lot of time talking about sports and the weather, but not about ideas to improve the business!
- You will never receive a person's second good idea until management has done something about the first one
- Exxon Baytown: more than 40 implemented improvements/person/year
  - North American and European average for all industries is 0.03 per person per year – American Productivity and Quality Center
- World-class performance results from engaging front-line people
- For world-class performance, engage every individual and empower everyone to make their best contribution

Best Team Practices

- Involve people affected by change to be a part of planning
- Create a no blame environment; employees speak up and take chances
- Give employees freedom to improve the process before standardizing
- Create process teams to monitor processes after standardization
- Let process teams create their own rules of engagement
- Stress teamwork above everything
- Remove metrics that discourage teamwork
- Encourage teams to focus on good in everyone with no back-biting!
- Strive to develop "High Performing Teams!"
- All want others to be the best they can be!
- Everyone cares for each other's success!

Example of Team Rules

Respect each other
- Listen well
- Cooperate
- Criticize with respect
- Go and return from break on time
- Report 5 minutes before start

Encourage each other to be their best

Lead by example

Do it right the first time
- Check standard operating procedure (SOP)

Clean up after yourself

Be responsible for cleaning your operator station

Replenish your station before you leave
- Check list of items to do

Allow ample time for replenishments

No silent disagreements

Courtesy: Harper Brush Manufacturing Company, Greenville, NC

Best Team Practices

- Encourage team rules and a fair workplace; transparency and fairness
- Encourage earning an honest day's wage for an honest day of labor
- Shun attitudes that kill ideas
- 10 Ways To Kill Ideas
  - Good idea! Now let's get back to reality
  - You have been hired only from your neck down!
  - Won't work! (Since when you became an expert?)
  - Sounds good, but has someone else done it?
  - Top management will never go for that
  - The supplier will never agree to that
  - The customer will never accept that
  - If it is not broken, why fix it
  - That is beyond our responsibility
  - That will make the other equipment obsolete

Veneer Technologies, Inc.
Lean Six-Sigma Yellow Belt (LSSYB) Training

Civility Matters at Work & Home!

- Hidden costs of incivility can be big!
- Incivility is a bug that can be contagious
  - Disrespect and rudeness
  - Mocking
  - Belittling
  - Teasing
  - Insensitivity
  - Offensive jokes
  - Backbiting and trying to get even
- Cisco conservatively estimates
  - Cost of incivility as $12 million per year

- Effect on those affected by uncivility
  - 66% cut back their efforts
  - 80% lost work time
  - 12% left their jobs
- Effect on witnesses
  - 25% had worse performance
  - 45% had fewer ideas
- Most incivility comes from a person with a higher status or a valued employee with talent

Source: TED Talk by Christine Porath, Management Researcher.

Reasons for Incivility

- Leaders think they will seem less leaderlike if they are too friendly
- Stress can drive bosses to become uncivil
- Civil leaders
  - Are twice as likely to be viewed as leaders by employees
  - Have 13% higher performance
  - Are viewed as warm and friendly
  - Are viewed as competent and smart
  - Are more productive, creative, helpful, happy and healthy, at work, at home and online

- Ways to enhance civility
- Thank people
  - Treat as if everyone is a volunteer
- Freely share the credit
- Listen attentively
- Ask questions in a humble way
- Acknowledge others
- Smile more

Improvement begins with self-improvement!

College of Engineering & Technology
EAST CAROLINA UNIVERSITY

Aim for Self Improvement

- How you think is everything
  - Be positive, don't drain your mind
  - Forget past mistakes, learn from them
  - Don't see other's mistakes as deliberate
- Plan and document your goals
  - Focus your time and resources
  - Don't let other's influence you
  - What people think of you is not your business!
  - Innovate! Be different.
- Take action! Have a bias for action
  - You can retreat if the path is not right!
  - Excessive analysis can lead to paralysis
  - Live life in the present
  - Make the best of all situations
- Learn till you die.
  - Act as if today is your last day; learn as if you are going to live forever…..MK Gandhi
  - Read, take classes, go back to school
- Be persistent and work hard
  - Success is a marathon; never give up!
  - Learn to analyze details
- Deal and communicate with people
  - All you want will come from someone!
  - Be humble; develop lasting friendships
  - Accept people and situations as they are; you cannot change what you don't control
- Be honest and dependable

Adapted from: IBD's Secrets of Success from Investor's Business Daily

---

Process Simulation

- Lego® airplanes
- Customer needs 25 planes
  - 13 Model Reds
  - 12 Model Greens
- Shift time = 6 minutes
- Must make in batches of 3
  - High reject rate: two fail out of a batch of 3

Model Red   Model Green

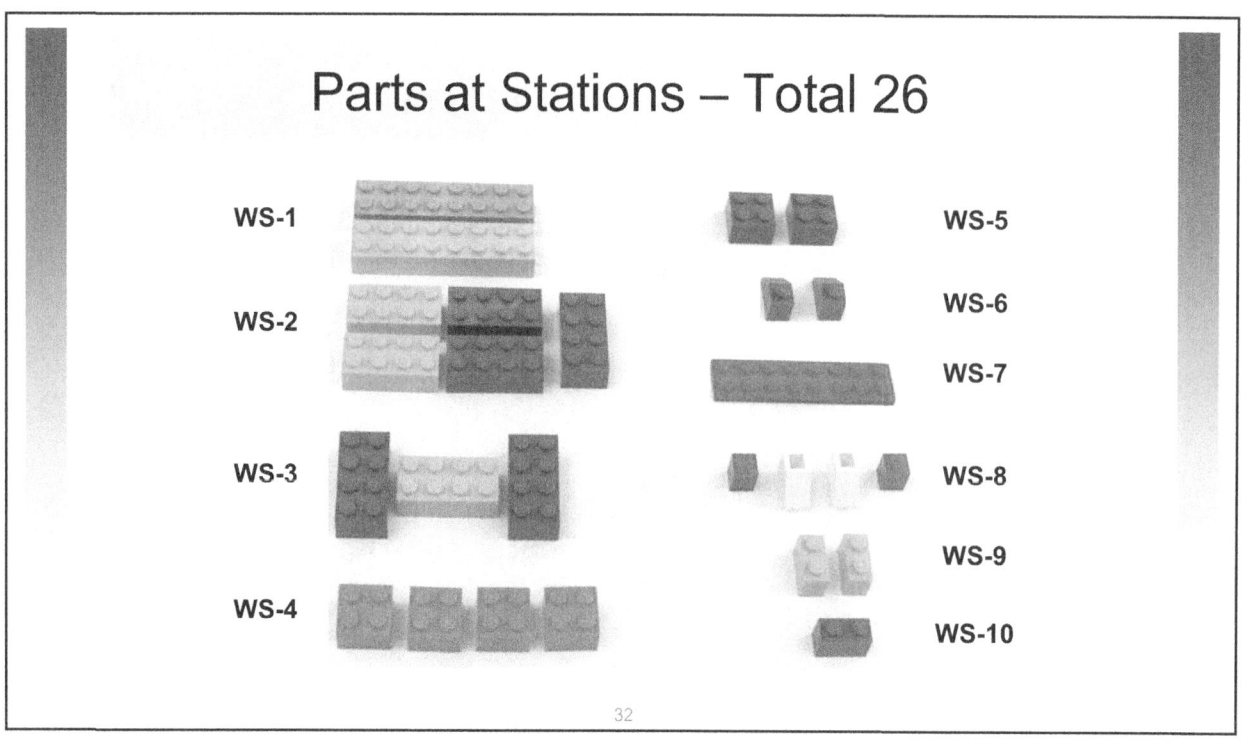

Veneer Technologies, Inc.
Lean Six-Sigma Yellow Belt (LSSYB) Training

Simulation Associates

Station #	Job Description	Assemblers
WS-1	Main members	2
WS-2	Wings	1
WS-3	Tail section	1
WS-4	Fuselage cabins	1
WS-5	Landing gear	1
WS-6	Cockpit	2
WS-7	Ailerons	1
WS-8	Jet engines	1
WS-9	Fuel tanks	1
WS-10	Rudder	1
WS-11	Inspection	1

Material Handlers	
Plant Manager	
Supervisor	
Sales manager	
CUSTOMER	

Parts at Stations – Total 26

- WS-1
- WS-2
- WS-3
- WS-4
- WS-5
- WS-6
- WS-7
- WS-8
- WS-9
- WS-10

College of Engineering & Technology
EAST CAROLINA UNIVERSITY

Veneer Technologies, Inc.
Lean Six-Sigma Yellow Belt (LSSYB) Training

WS-1: Main Members

Operators	
1	
2	

WS-2: Wings

Operation 1

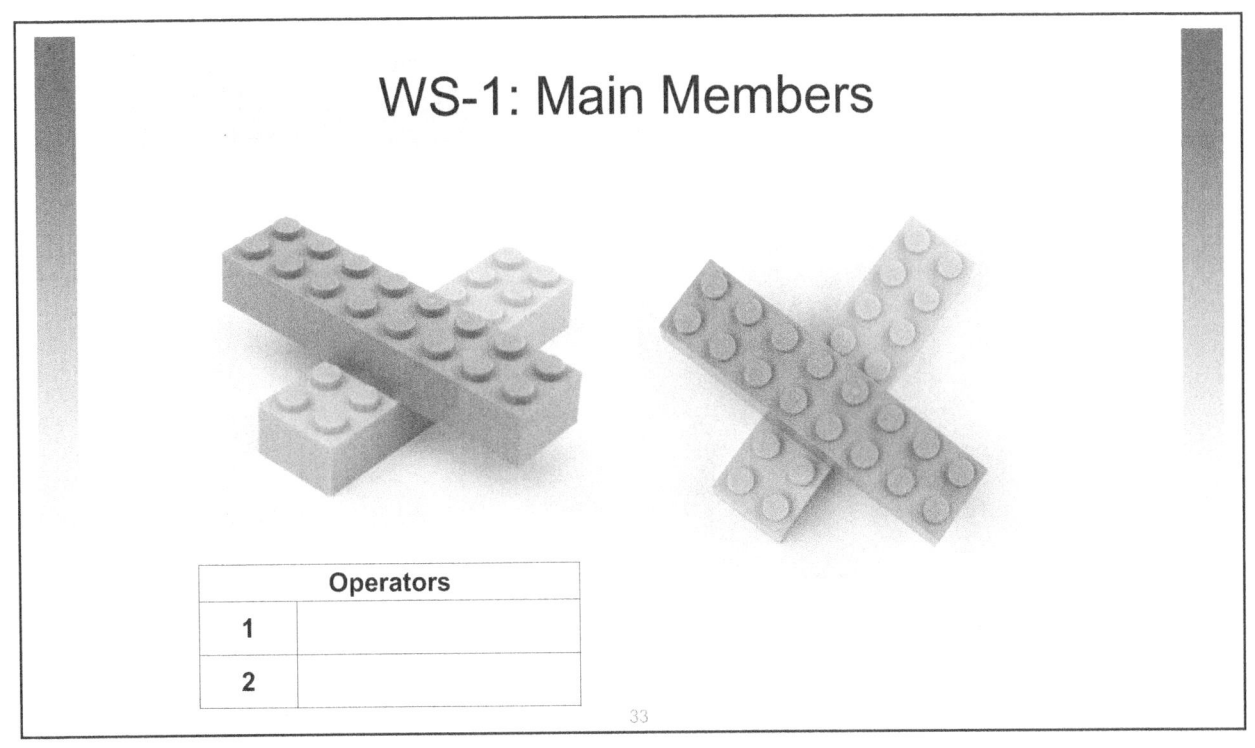

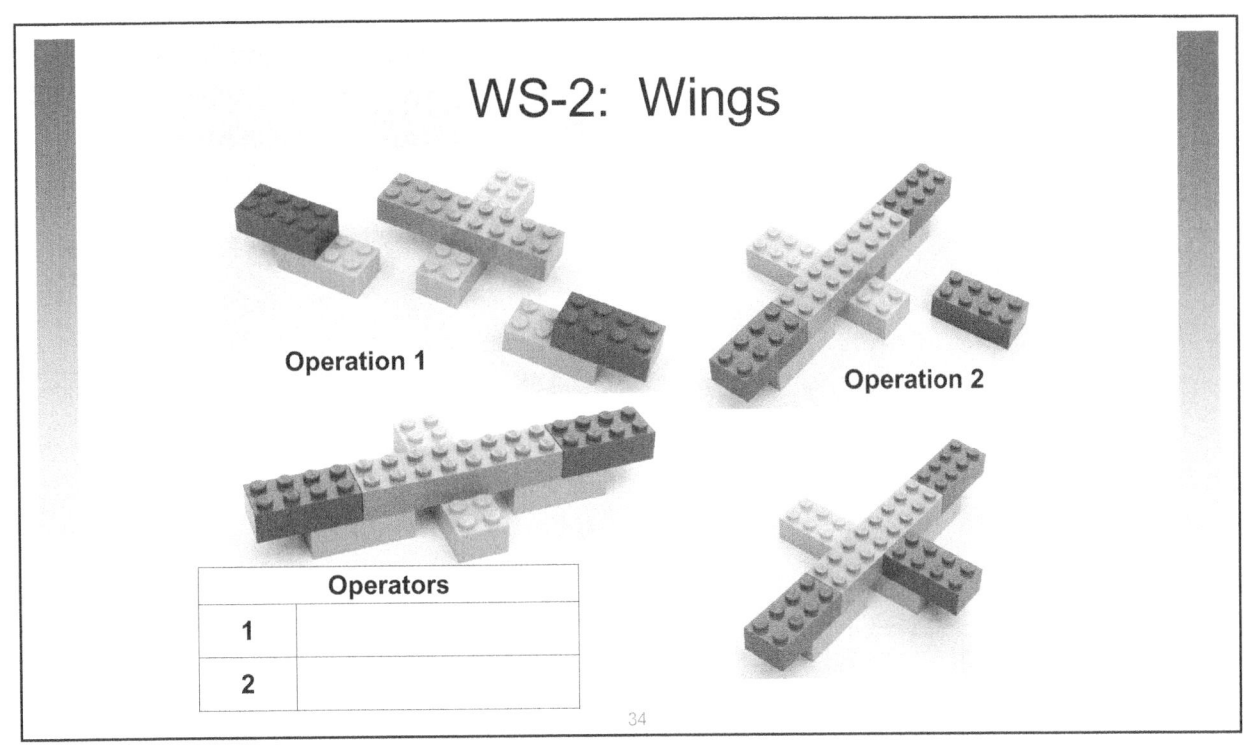

Operation 2

Operators	
1	
2	

College of Engineering & Technology
EAST CAROLINA UNIVERSITY

Veneer Technologies, Inc.
Lean Six-Sigma Yellow Belt (LSSYB) Training

18

WS-3: Tail Section

Operators	
1	
2	

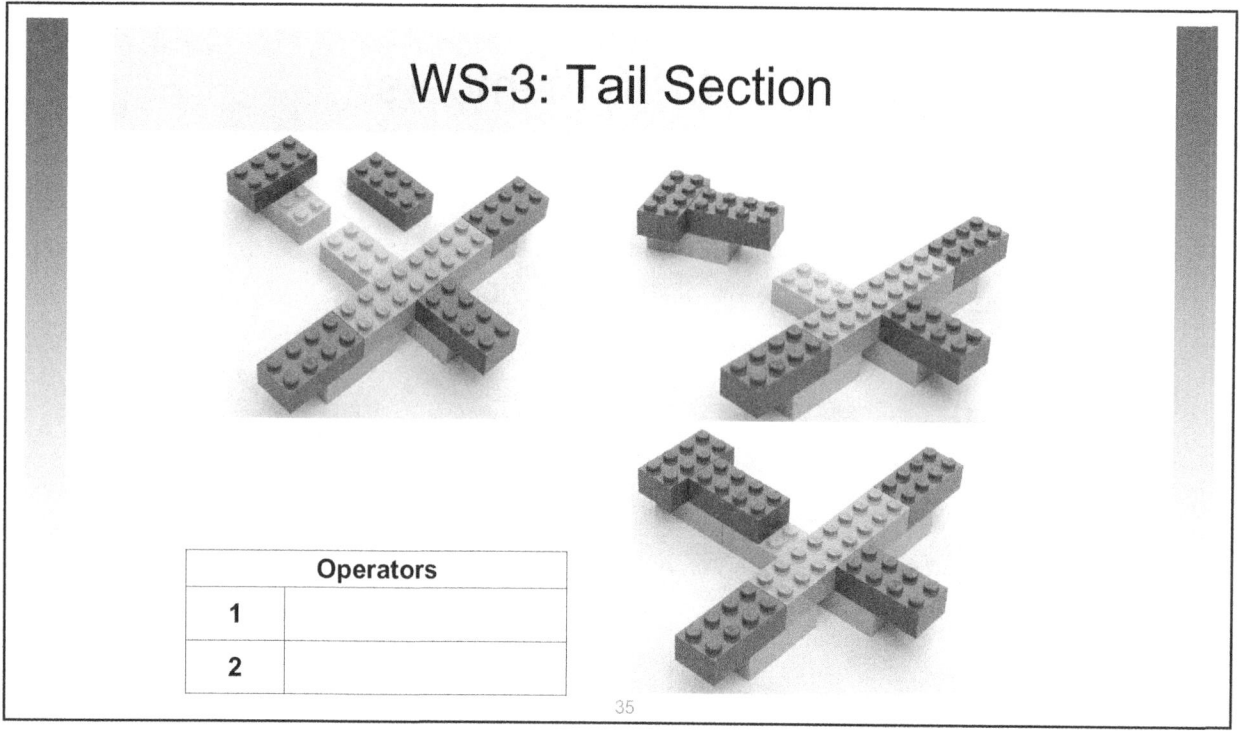

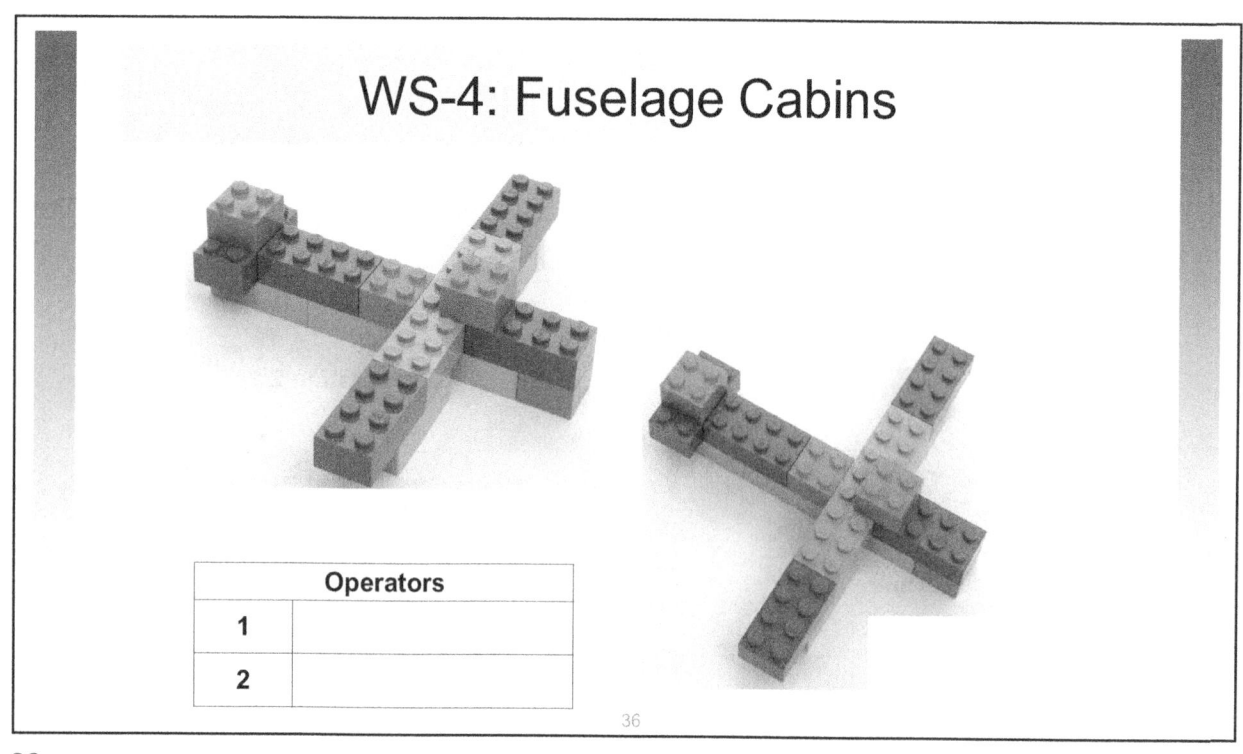

WS-4: Fuselage Cabins

Operators	
1	
2	

College of Engineering & Technology
EAST CAROLINA UNIVERSITY

Veneer Technologies, Inc.
Lean Six-Sigma Yellow Belt (LSSYB) Training

WS-5: Landing Gear

	Operators
1	
2	

WS-6: Cockpit

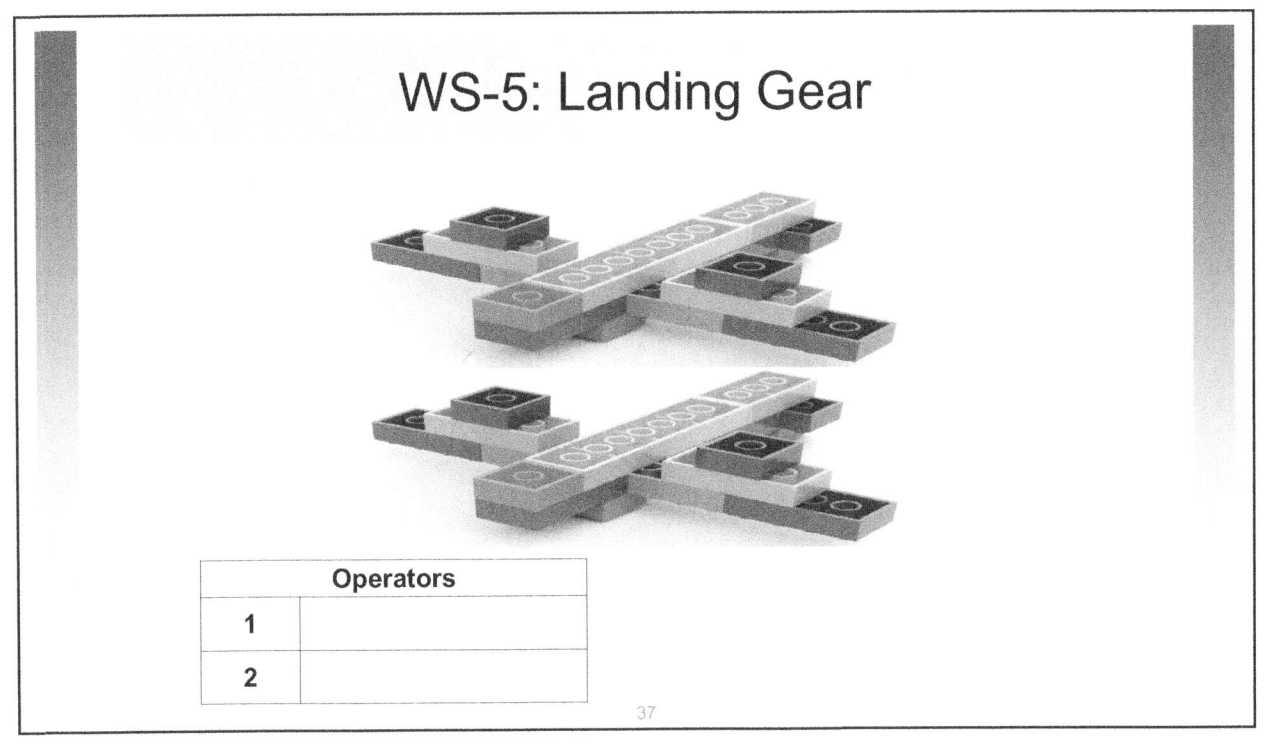

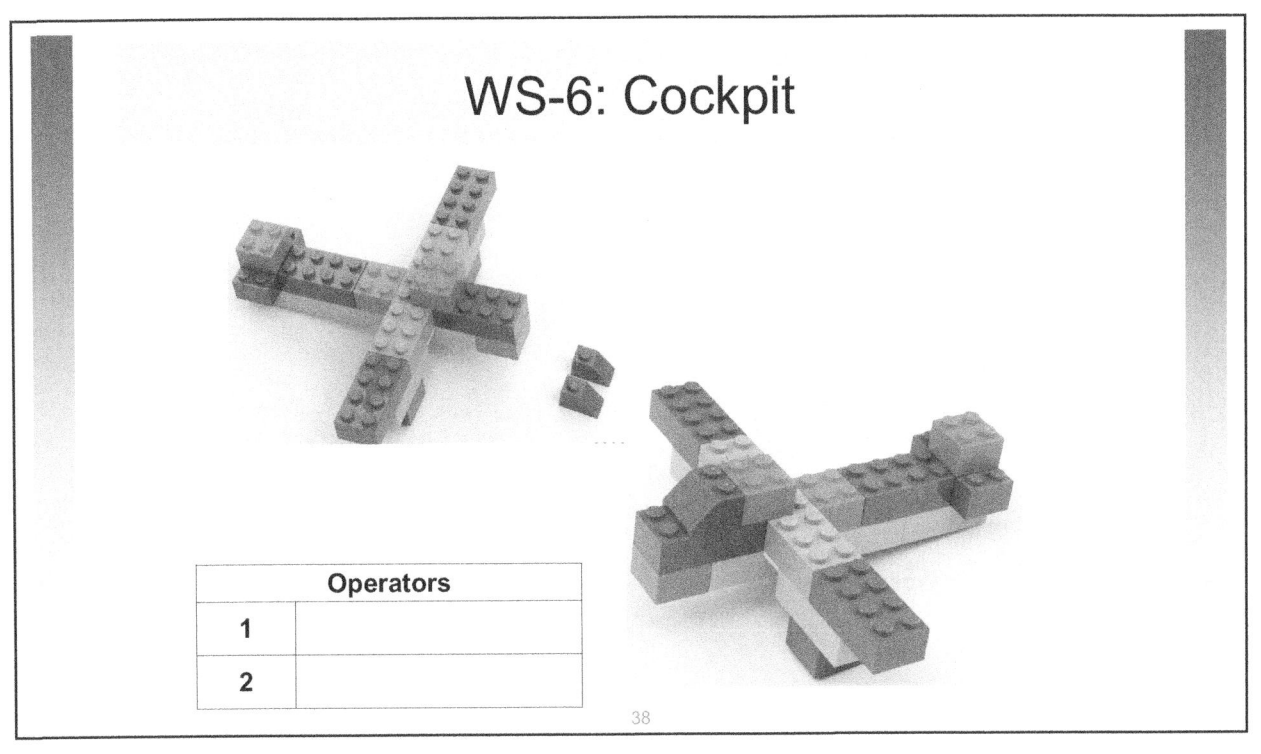

	Operators
1	
2	

College of Engineering & Technology
EAST CAROLINA UNIVERSITY

Veneer Technologies, Inc.
Lean Six-Sigma Yellow Belt (LSSYB) Training

WS-7: Aileron

	Operators
1	
2	

WS-8: Jet Engines

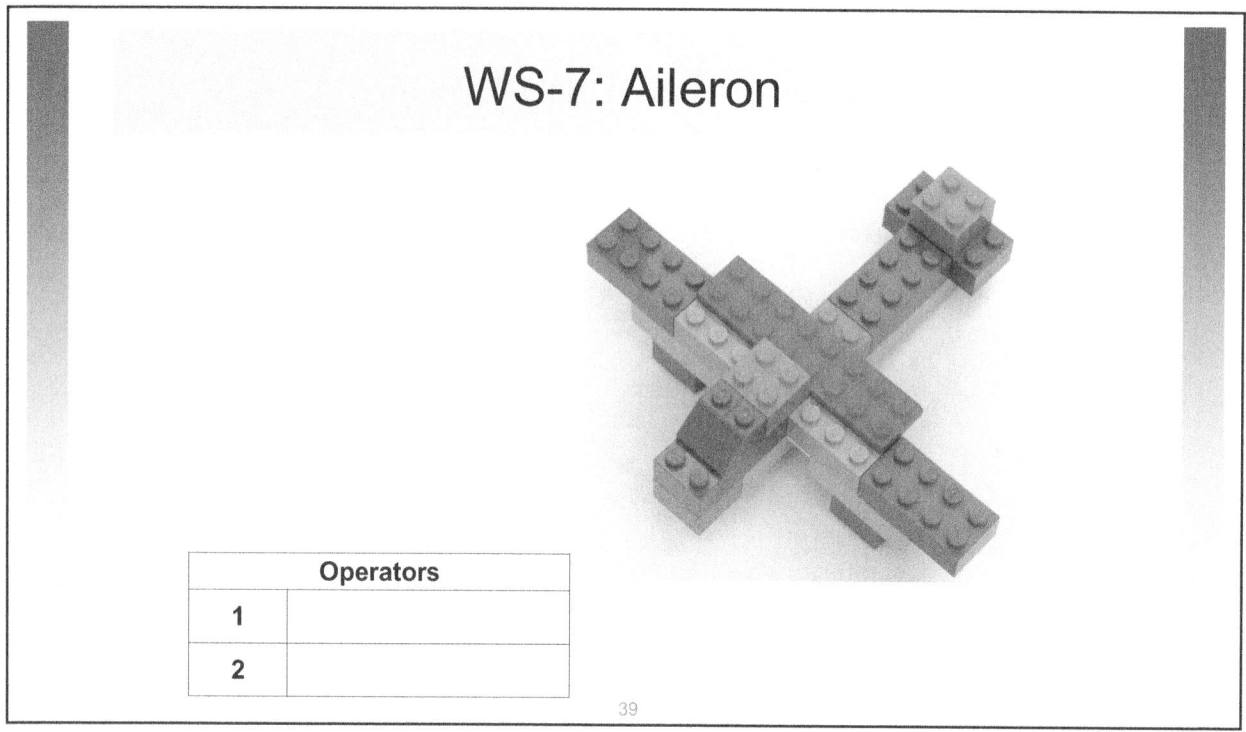

	Operators
1	
2	

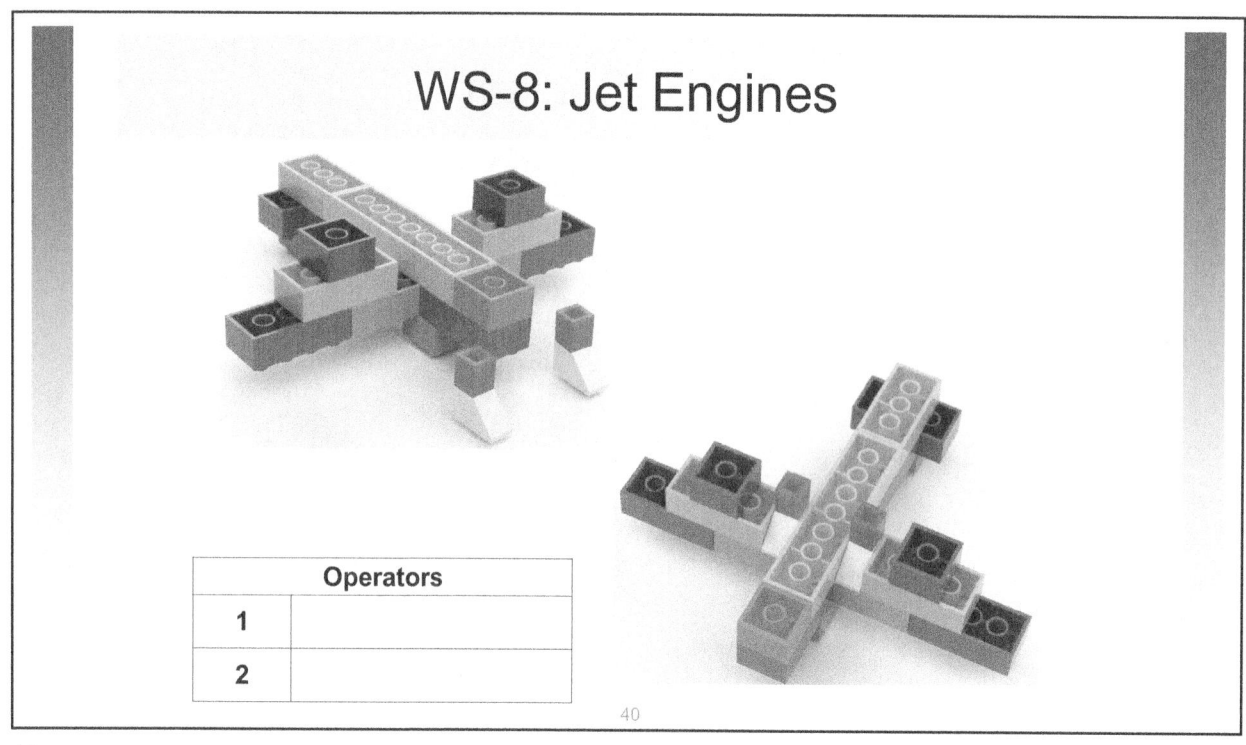

College of Engineering & Technology
EAST CAROLINA UNIVERSITY

Veneer Technologies, Inc.
Lean Six-Sigma Yellow Belt (LSSYB) Training

WS-9: Fuel Tanks

Operators	
1	
2	

WS-10: Rudder

Operators	
1	
2	

College of Engineering & Technology
EAST CAROLINA UNIVERSITY

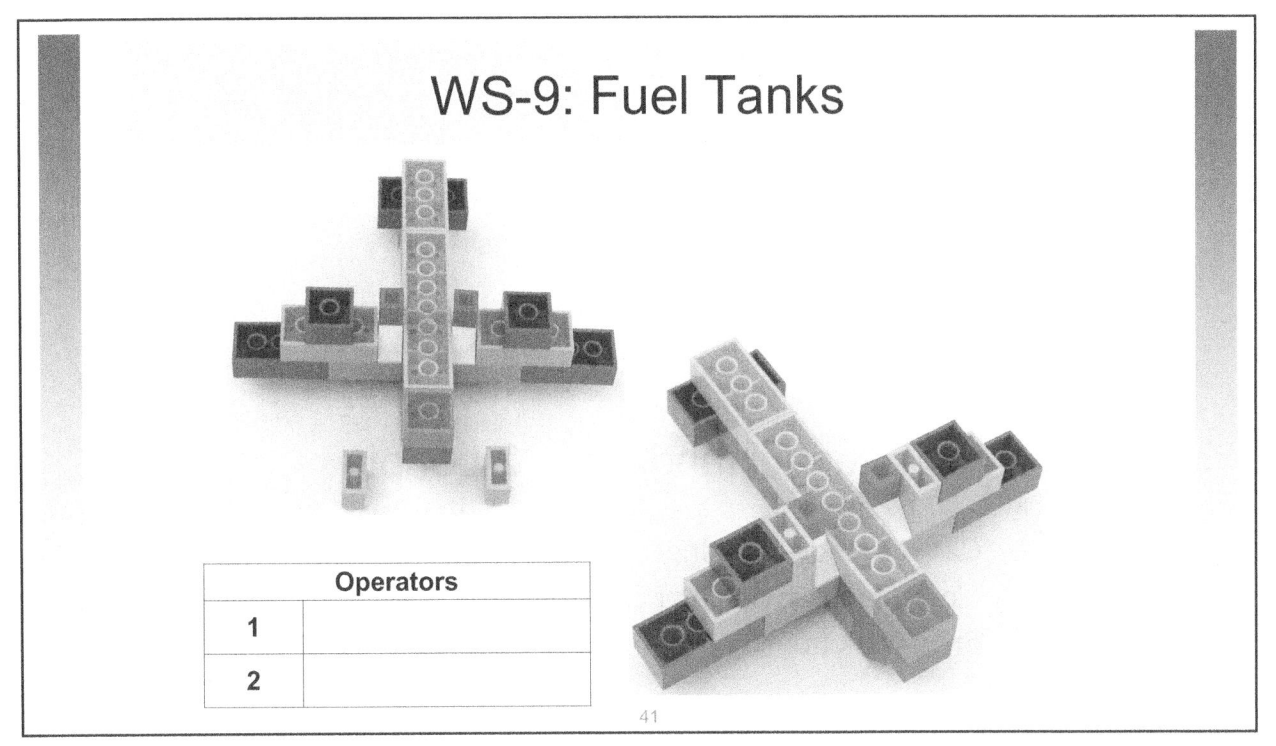

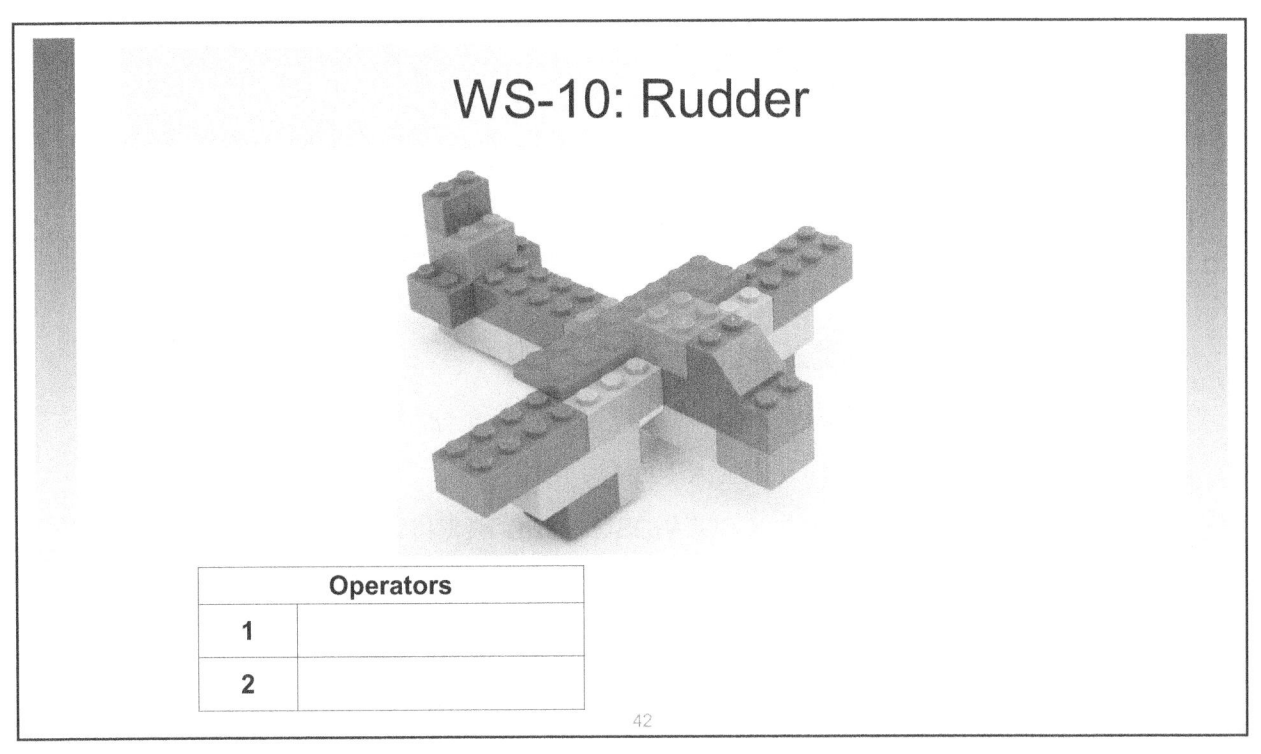

WS-11: Inspector

- Check parts are in correct color & orientation
- Use gage to check gap between parts
- Ring bell when product is good
- Inspector name: _____

Material Handlers – 2 people

- Can only move material
- Move planes in batch of 3
- Bring work from storage

Operators	
1	
2	

Rules for Round 1

- Work time: <u>Until one good airplane is made</u>
- If one is rejected from batch of 3, move the remaining good ones
- NO PRE-ASSEMBLY ALLOWED
- No complaining about bad training!
- Keep working – no thinking or fixing!
  - You are paid to work not waste time in thinking!
  - You are paid to keep the process moving, not fix quality problems

Veneer Technologies, Inc.
Lean Six-Sigma Yellow Belt (LSSYB) Training

Round 1 Results

Station #	Job Description	Inventory Created	# of Rejects
WS-1	Main members		
WS-2	Wings		
WS-3	Tail section		
WS-4	Fuselage cabins		
WS-5	Landing gear		
WS-6	Cockpit		
WS-7	Ailerons		
WS-8	Jet engines		
WS-9	Fuel tanks		
WS-10	Rudder		
WS-11	Inspection		
	Total		

Airplanes made: 1

Time to complete 1 airplane = Lead time = _____ secs

Metrics for Round 1

Process Metrics	Round 1
Time to make one airplane	
Airplanes made	
Total inventory in process	
Airplanes rejected	
Number of people	
Productivity: airplanes / # people	

Identify opportunities for improvement

College of Engineering & Technology
EAST CAROLINA UNIVERSITY

Veneer Technologies, Inc.
Lean Six-Sigma Yellow Belt (LSSYB) Training

Improvement Ideas

1. .
2. .
3. .
4. .
5. .
6. .
7. .
8. .
9. .

Defining a Process

- A process converts inputs into outputs
- Inputs / outputs can be parts, services or information
- A process can have multiple activities
- Processes need to have a fixed start & end time
- All work can be defined as a process
- Processes evolve and rarely are designed
- Customers only want to pay for what parts of the process provide them value

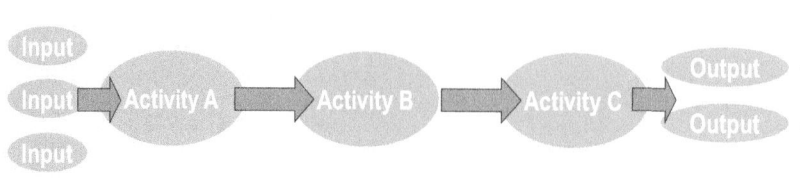

http://www.aplcresearch.com/Baton%20passing.jpg

Input → Activity A → Activity B → Activity C → Output

College of Engineering & Technology
EAST CAROLINA UNIVERSITY

Veneer Technologies, Inc.
Lean Six-Sigma Yellow Belt (LSSYB) Training

Process Improvement Step 1

- Reduce lead time first. Time between start and end. Time customer waits.

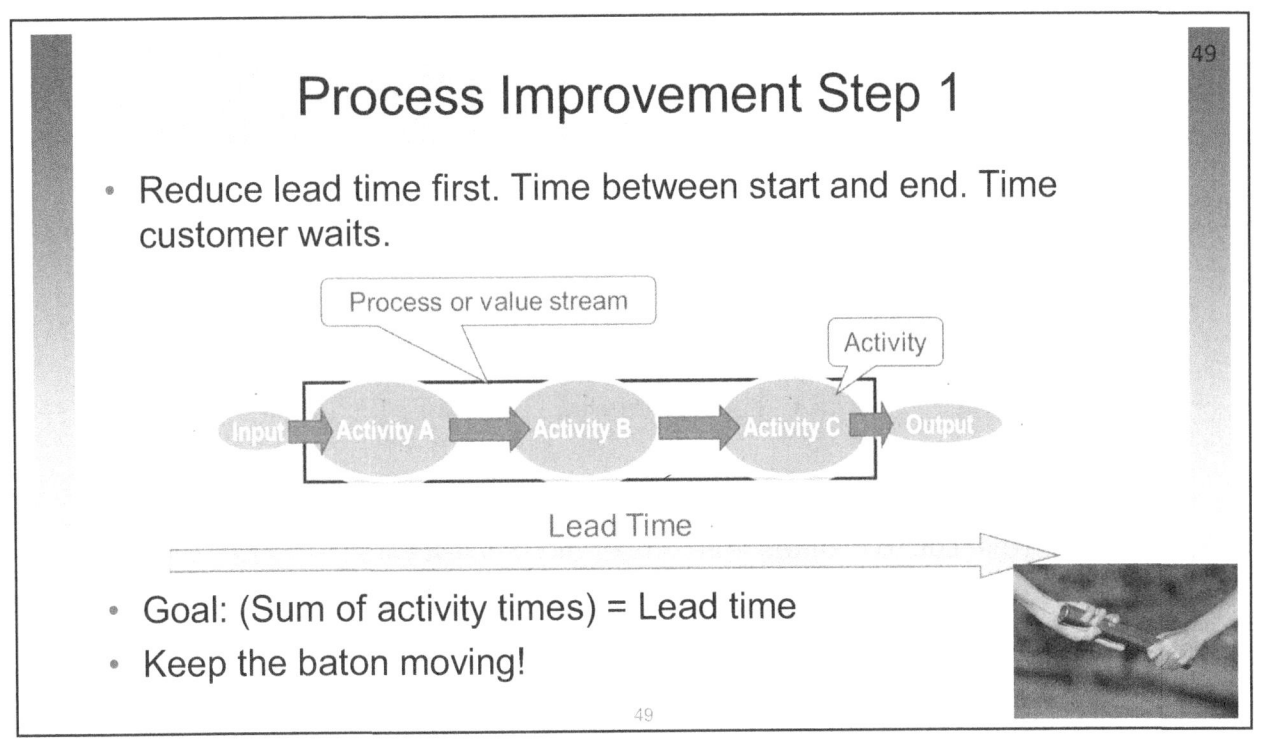

- Goal: (Sum of activity times) = Lead time
- Keep the baton moving!

Percentage Value Added Time (%VAT)

- Also called process cycle efficiency (PCE)
- Find VAT ratio and %VAT for process.
- VAT ratio = (sum of activity times) / (lead time)
- %VAT = VAT ratio x 100.
- When, (sum of activity times) = (lead time), %VAT = 100%
- What is the VAT ratio and %VAT for process shown if lead time = 8 hours

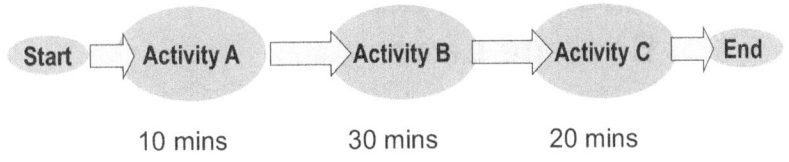

Start → Activity A (10 mins) → Activity B (30 mins) → Activity C (20 mins) → End

- VAT ratio = (sum of activity times) / (lead time),
- For most processes %VAT is between 5% - 25%

College of Engineering & Technology
EAST CAROLINA UNIVERSITY

Veneer Technologies, Inc.
Lean Six-Sigma Yellow Belt (LSSYB) Training

Process Improvement Step 2

- If sum of activity times is not acceptable as the lead time, consider reducing activity times
- Lead time needed = 50 mins
- What can we do?

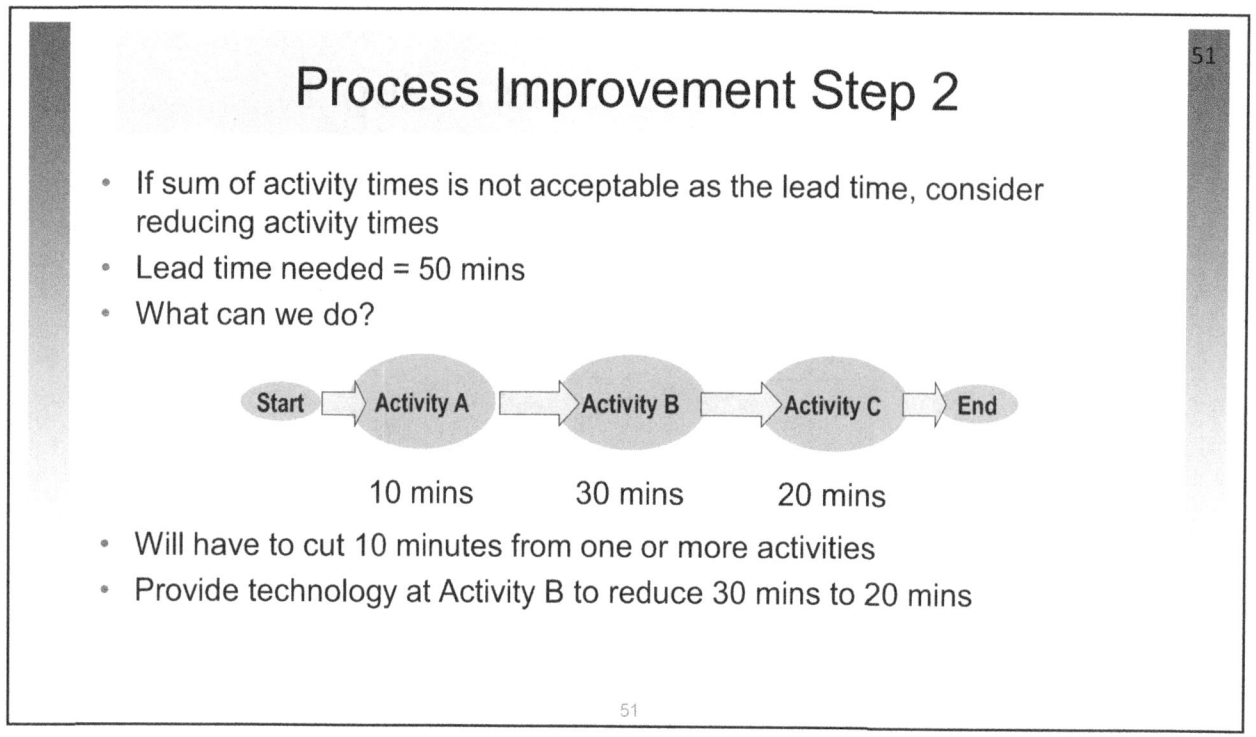

Start → Activity A (10 mins) → Activity B (30 mins) → Activity C (20 mins) → End

- Will have to cut 10 minutes from one or more activities
- Provide technology at Activity B to reduce 30 mins to 20 mins

---

Toast Kaizen

- I — Inventory/Storage Waste
- M — Motion Waste
- T — Transportation Waste
- W — Waiting Waste
- People Waste
- O — Over-Production
- D — Defects Waste
- O — Over-Processing

TIM WOOD Helps Processes Become Lean

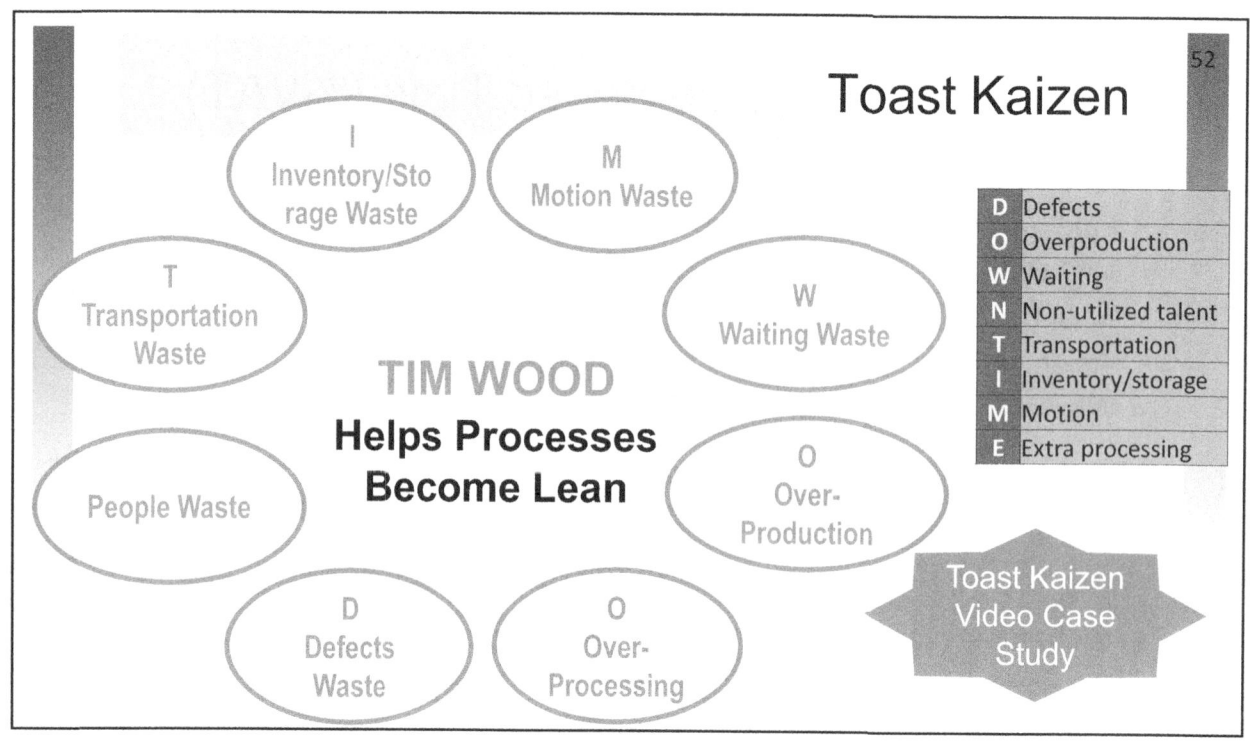

D	Defects
O	Overproduction
W	Waiting
N	Non-utilized talent
T	Transportation
I	Inventory/storage
M	Motion
E	Extra processing

Toast Kaizen Video Case Study

College of Engineering & Technology
EAST CAROLINA UNIVERSITY

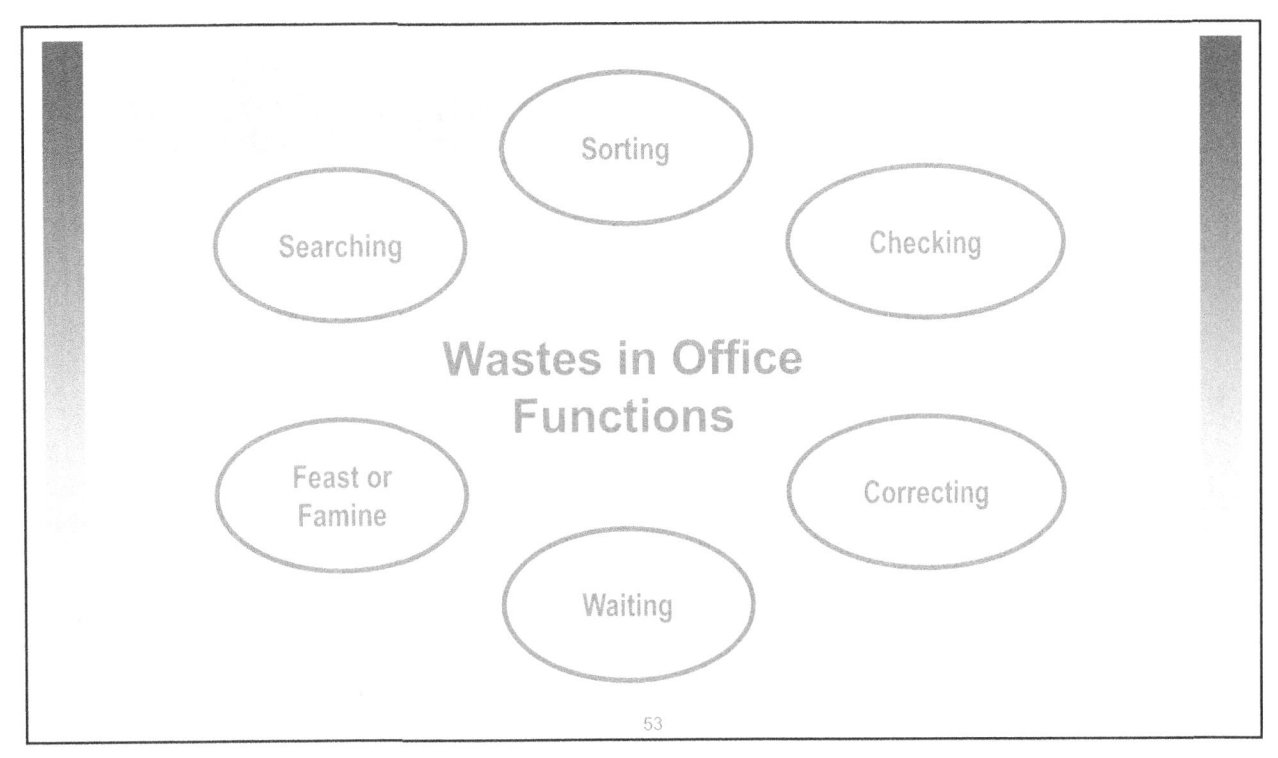

Veneer Technologies, Inc.
Lean Six-Sigma Yellow Belt (LSSYB) Training

Wastes in Office Functions

- Sorting
- Searching
- Checking
- Feast or Famine
- Correcting
- Waiting

Convert Processes into Value Streams

- Define process start and end moments
- Track lead time
  - Time between start & end moments
  - Time for which customer is waiting!

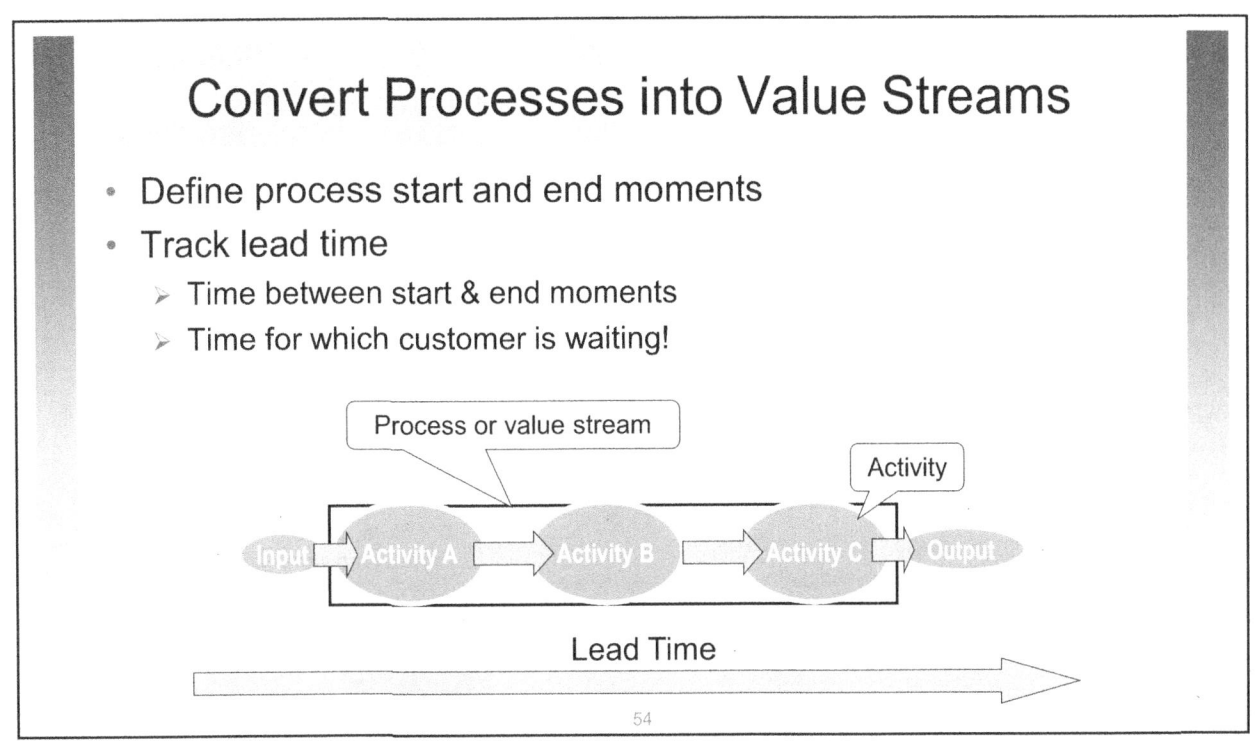

Input → Activity A → Activity B → Activity C → Output

Process or value stream | Activity | Lead Time

College of Engineering & Technology
EAST CAROLINA UNIVERSITY

The Value Stream

- Process that increasingly adds value to output from the customer's point of view
- If you can't describe what you are doing as a process, you don't know what you're doing.   W. Edwards Deming

  - Flow of most work is difficult to see
  - Invisible work can't be improved

Issues with Traditional Processes

Process

RFQ → Customer Service → Engineering → Quoting → Customer

Purchasing

- Organized as functional depts.
- Work travels to multiple depts.
- Employees responsible for dept. function only
- Long lead-times & large queues of WIP
- Lengthy problem resolution cycles
- Handoffs create mistakes and loss of information
- Checkpoints are needed to identify mistakes

- Employees are unaware of whole system—unable to improve
- Local measures & conflicting dept. goals
- Approvals required to control fragmented work

Source: Hyer & Wemmerlov, Reorganizing the Factory: Competing through Cellular Manufacturing

Waste of Human Talent

- Not using people's mental, and creative skills
  - Limiting people to functional responsibilities: focus on defined tasks
  - No encouragement for developing new skills
  - Unwillingness to consider an idea or experiment with new ideas
  - Limiting the opportunity for all people to be problem solvers
- Remedies:
  - Consider sharing benefits and information
  - Consider profit sharing and reward structures
  - Develop people; provide training
  - Encourage teamwork, and team recognition
  - Invest in continuous improvement culture
  - Empower employees; promote from within!

Process Time Definitions

- Lead time (L/T)
  - Time for which the customer is waiting
  - Time from order receipt to delivery
  - Time between process start and end moments
- Activity time (A/T) or operation time (O/T) or touch time (T/T)
  - Time to complete one cycle of an activity
- Cycle time (C/T)
  - Average time taken by an output for an activity
  - Cycle time = (Activity time) divided by (number of outputs produced in one cycle) of an activity

Veneer Technologies, Inc.
Lean Six-Sigma Yellow Belt (LSSYB) Training

Activity Time (A/T) & Cycle Time (C/T)

- Activity time = 10 minutes
- On completion, 4 outputs are produced
- What is the C/T for the activity?
- C/T = (Activity time) / (# of outputs)
- C/T = _____ / _____
- Test yourself:
- Activity time = 20 minutes per part per station
- There are 8 stations
- What is the rate of production or C/T for operation?

4 outputs in 10 mins

4 stations, each taking 10 mins

Value Added Tasks

- **Value-Added Task (VAT)**
  - Customer is happy to pay for the task
- **Non-Value-Added Task (NVAT)**
  - Redesign task – pass savings to customers
    - ✓ Eliminate the task, merge with upstream (previous) task, merge with downstream (next) task
- **Business Value Added/Sustaining Tasks**
  - Required due to the nature of the process
  - Business reasons, laws or regulations or to reduce financial risk / liability

Input → Activity A → Activity B → Activity C → Output

College of Engineering & Technology
EAST CAROLINA UNIVERSITY

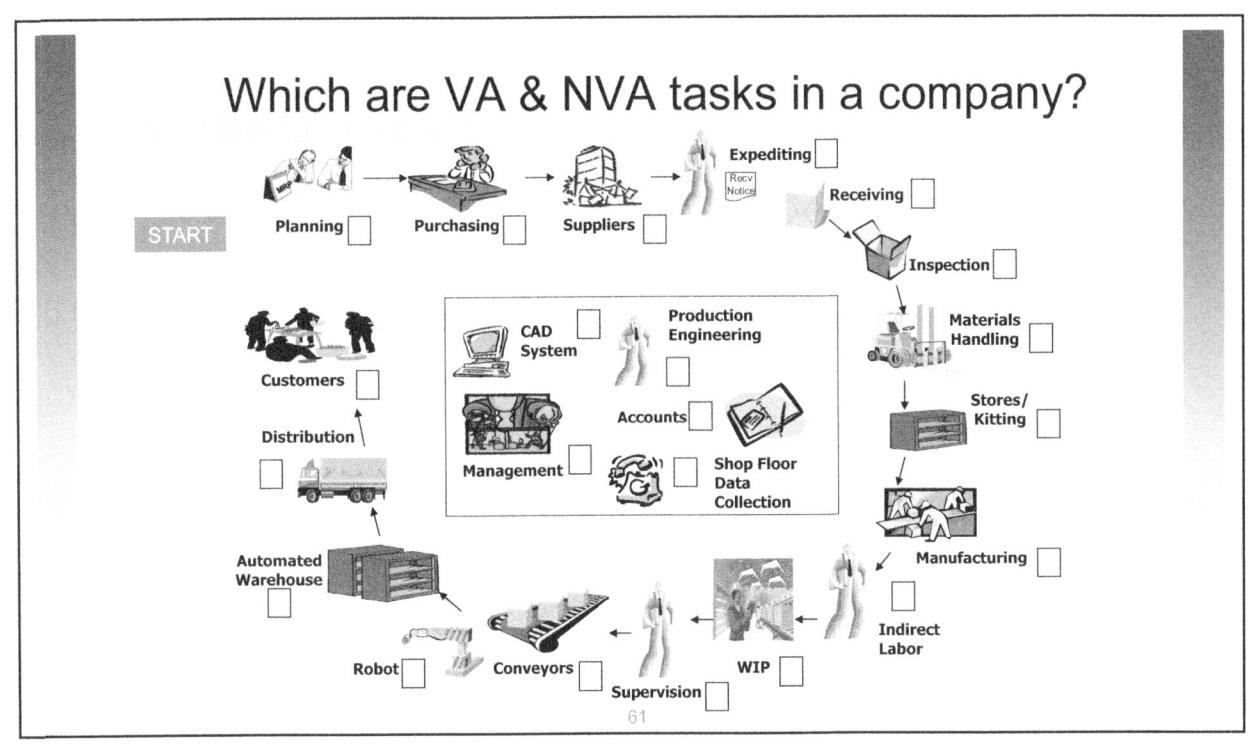

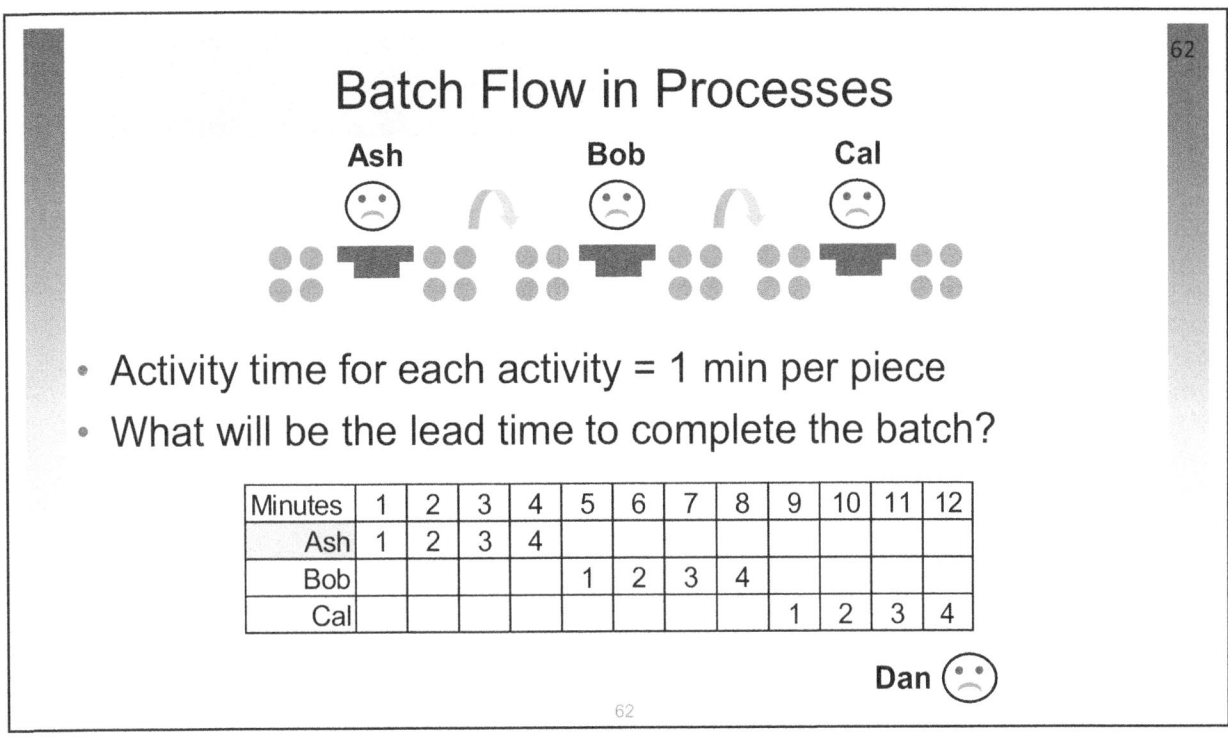

Veneer Technologies, Inc.
Lean Six-Sigma Yellow Belt (LSSYB) Training

Which are VA & NVA tasks in a company?

START → Planning → Purchasing → Suppliers → Expediting → Receiving → Inspection → Materials Handling → Stores/Kitting → Manufacturing → Indirect Labor → WIP → Supervision → Conveyors → Robot → Automated Warehouse → Distribution → Customers

Central box: CAD System, Production Engineering, Accounts, Management, Shop Floor Data Collection

Batch Flow in Processes

Ash → Bob → Cal

- Activity time for each activity = 1 min per piece
- What will be the lead time to complete the batch?

Minutes	1	2	3	4	5	6	7	8	9	10	11	12
Ash	1	2	3	4								
Bob					1	2	3	4				
Cal									1	2	3	4

Dan

College of Engineering & Technology
EAST CAROLINA UNIVERSITY

Veneer Technologies, Inc.
Lean Six-Sigma Yellow Belt (LSSYB) Training

Continuous Flow
Complete one, move one (COMO), Make one, move one (MOMO)

Ash Bob Cal

- Activity time for each activity = 1 min per piece
- What will be the lead time to complete the batch?

Minutes	1	2	3	4	5	6	7	8	9	10	11	12
Ash	1	2	3	4								
Bob		1	2	3	4							
Cal			1	2	3	4						

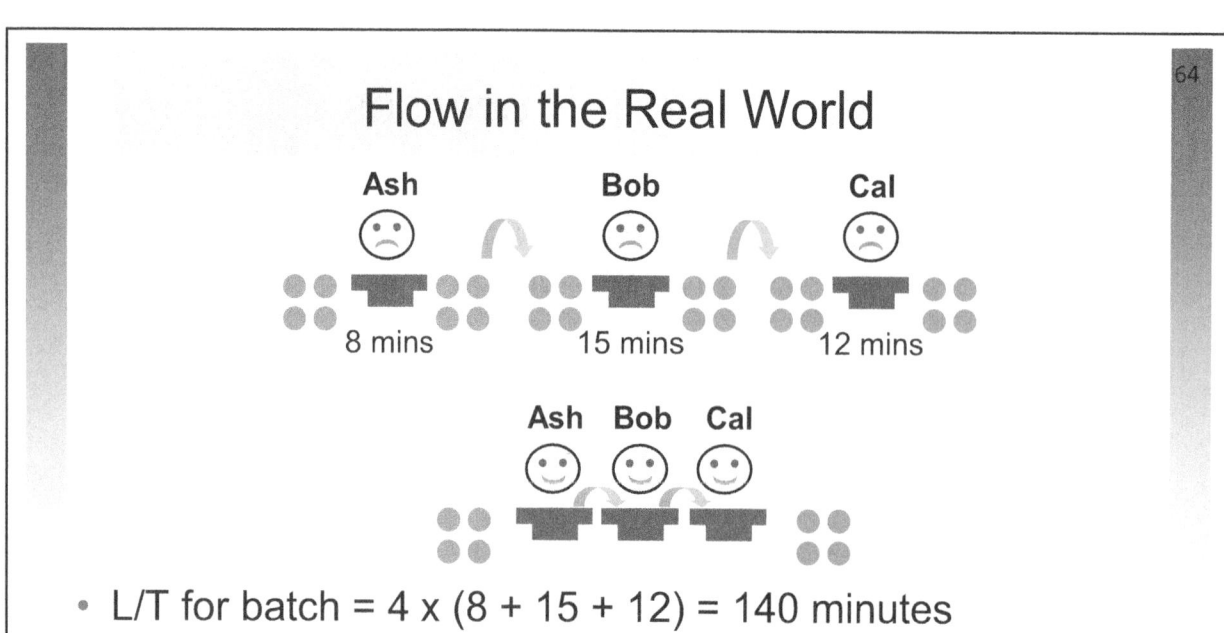

Flow in the Real World

Ash — 8 mins
Bob — 15 mins
Cal — 12 mins

- L/T for batch = 4 x (8 + 15 + 12) = 140 minutes
- L/T for MOMO = 8 + 15 + 12 + (3 x 15) = 80 minutes

College of Engineering & Technology
EAST CAROLINA UNIVERSITY

Veneer Technologies, Inc.
Lean Six-Sigma Yellow Belt (LSSYB) Training

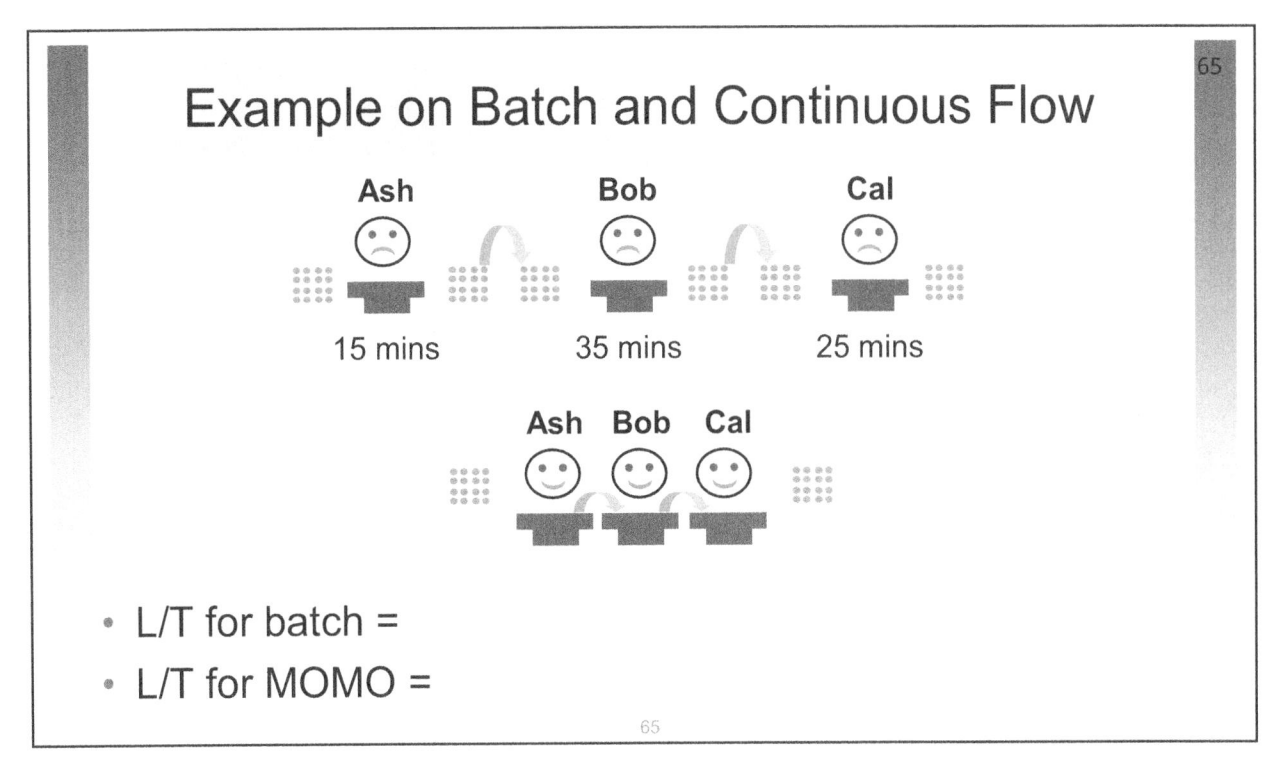

Example on Batch and Continuous Flow

Ash — 15 mins
Bob — 35 mins
Cal — 25 mins

Ash Bob Cal

- L/T for batch =
- L/T for MOMO =

Kanban

- Japanese word for "signal" or sign
- Triggers flow of output
- Self-adjusting, visual system for inventory
- Used for tying activities together in a process
- Based on the supermarket principle
- Best is no Kanban and one-piece flow
- Works under strict discipline
- Toyota moves billions of dollars worth of inventory

People make a system erratic; Without rules and discipline!

College of Engineering & Technology
EAST CAROLINA UNIVERSITY

Veneer Technologies, Inc.
Lean Six-Sigma Yellow Belt (LSSYB) Training

Pull System Model Using Kanban

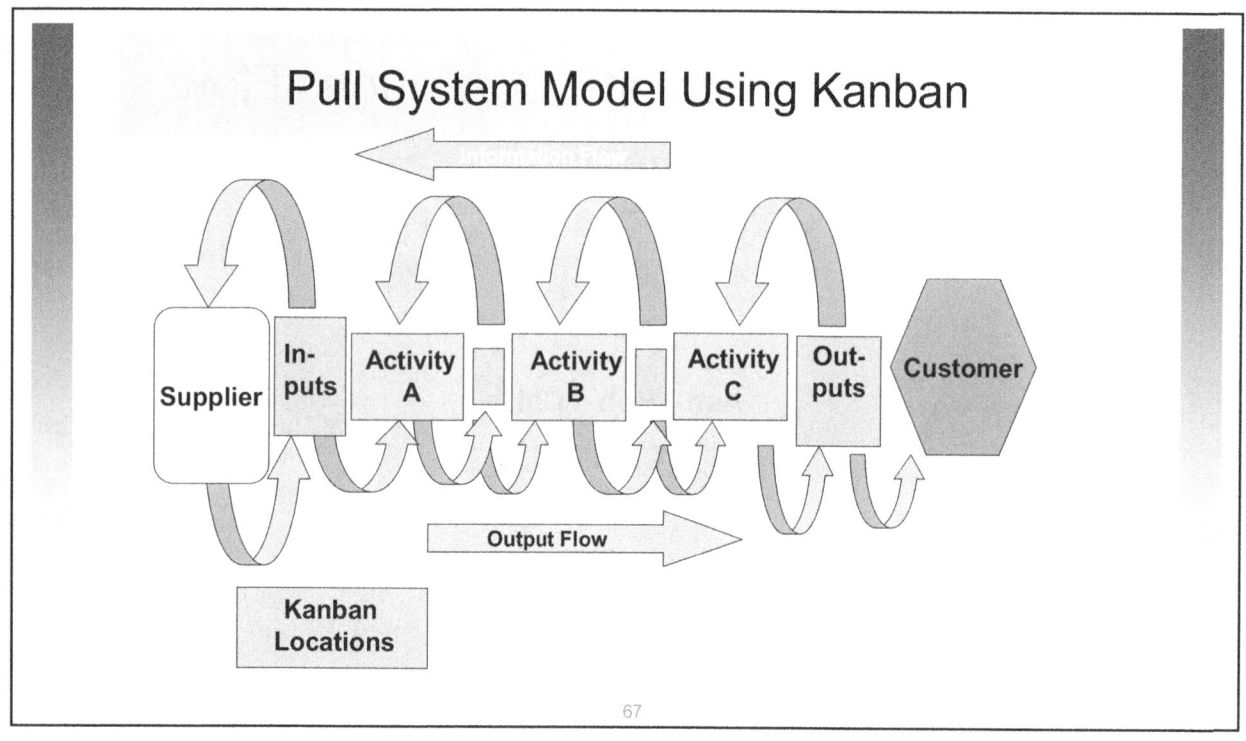

Information Flow

Supplier → In-puts → Activity A → Activity B → Activity C → Out-puts → Customer

Output Flow

Kanban Locations

Theory of Constraints

1. Identify the Constraint
2. Exploit the Constraint (Get maximum output)
3. Subordinate everything to the Constraint
4. Elevate the Constraint (Run through breaks, reduce setup times, etc.)
5. Repeat for the new Constraint

Systems are like chains.

Reliability of a system is the reliability of the least reliable component in the system.

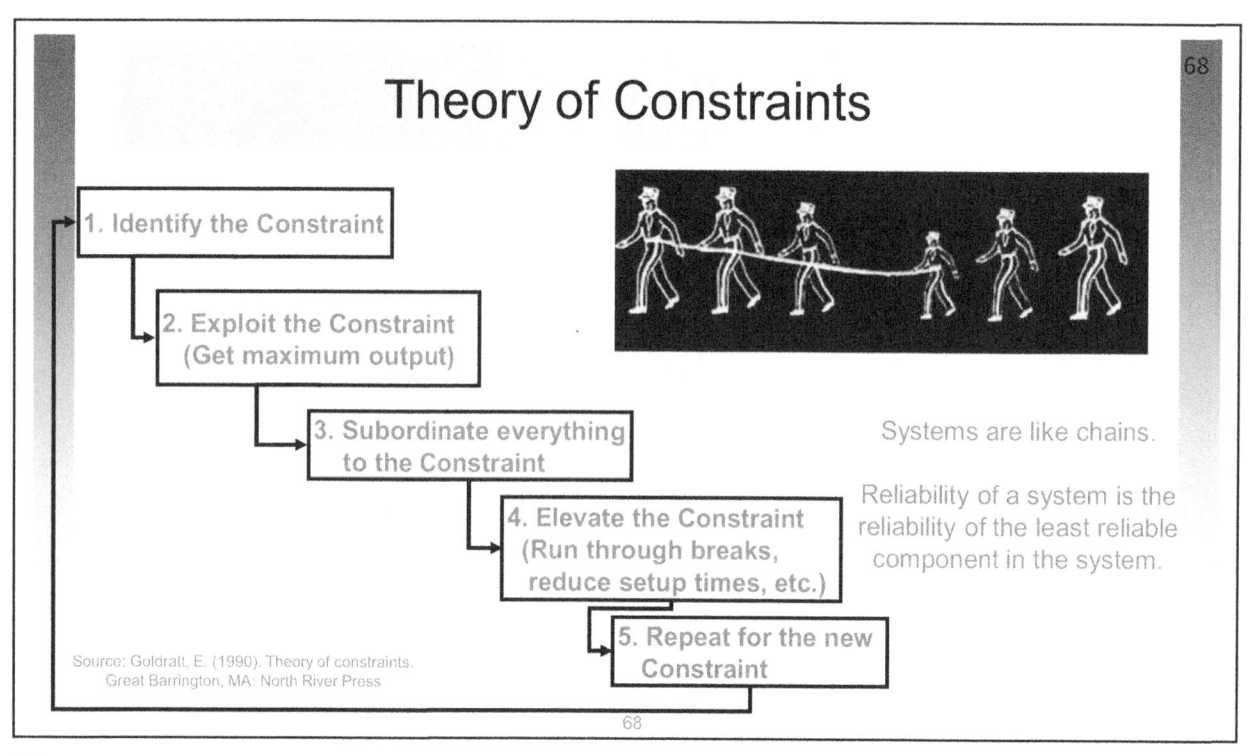

Source: Goldratt, E. (1990). Theory of constraints. Great Barrington, MA: North River Press

College of Engineering & Technology
EAST CAROLINA UNIVERSITY

Concept of Takt Time

- Align activities using a drumbeat / metronome
- Drumbeat: average rate customer needs output
- Average rate at which process should produce 1 output

- Customer needs 25 outputs in 6 minutes
- The rate of customer need = (6 mins x 60 secs) / 25

  Takt Time = 14.4 seconds / output

$$\text{Takt Time} = \frac{\text{Effective working time (per period)}}{\text{Customer requirement (per period)}}$$

Concept of Takt Time

- **If customer needs 1,200 outputs in a day, what should be the Takt time?**
- Assume the process runs for a 12-hour shift with ½ an hour for a lunch break.

- Customer needs 1200 outputs in (11.5 x 60) minutes
- The rate of customer need =
-        Takt Time =

$$\text{Takt Time} = \frac{\text{Effective working time (per period)}}{\text{Customer requirement (per period)}}$$

Veneer Technologies, Inc.
Lean Six-Sigma Yellow Belt (LSSYB) Training

Activity Efficiency for a Process

- Make every minute of every employee productive by designing and monitoring processes!
- Goals:
  - To design a well-balanced process
  - To monitor how well employees are performing
    - Working as an aligned team
    - More important to be aligned than right!

Example of Activity Efficiency for a Process

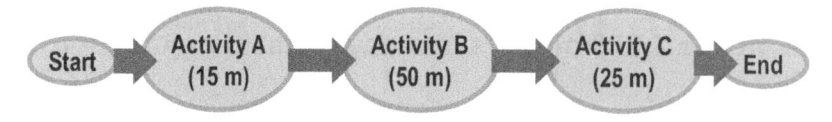

Start → Activity A (15 m) → Activity B (50 m) → Activity C (25 m) → End

- Sum of activity times = 90 mins
- Each activity is manned by one person
- Working day is 8 hours with 2, 10-minute breaks
- Working time = (8 hrs x 60 mins) – (2 x 10) = 460 mins
- Total person-minutes in the cell = 3 x 460 = 1380 mins
- Ideal expected output = (available time) / (time for one output)
- Ideal expected output = 1380 / 90 = 15.33 units

College of Engineering & Technology
EAST CAROLINA UNIVERSITY

Veneer Technologies, Inc.
Lean Six-Sigma Yellow Belt (LSSYB) Training

Example of an unprimed process

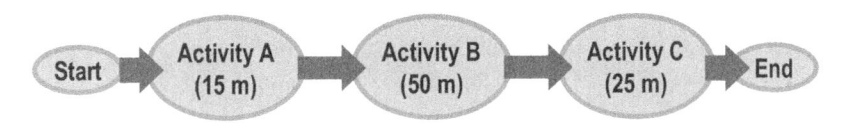

Start → Activity A (15 m) → Activity B (50 m) → Activity C (25 m) → End

- First output will take 15 + 50 + 25 = 90 mins
- Second output will take?
- (a) 90 mins; (b) 25 mins; (c) 50 mins

- Infrequently done processes
- At end of the day, process is empty
- Perishable outputs; custom tooling; TV dinners; surgery

Activity Efficiency for an unprimed process

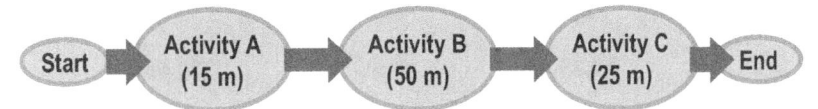

Start → Activity A (15 m) → Activity B (50 m) → Activity C (25 m) → End

- The first output will be available in 90 mins
- The C/T for the process will be 50 mins because Activity B is the bottleneck
- In the remaining (460 − 90) = 370 mins, we can get (370 / 50) = 7.4 units
- In a workday we get (1 + 7.4) = 8.4 units

- Note in this scenario, we started with no outputs in between activities or with an unprimed process

College of Engineering & Technology
EAST CAROLINA UNIVERSITY

Veneer Technologies, Inc.
Lean Six-Sigma Yellow Belt (LSSYB) Training

Example of a primed process

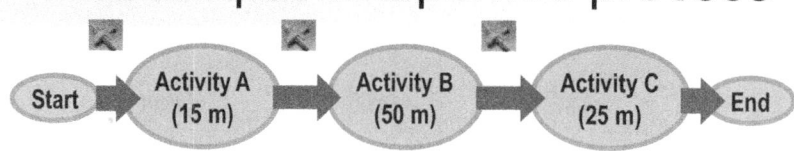

Start → Activity A (15 m) → Activity B (50 m) → Activity C (25 m) → End

- First output will take 25 mins (time for last activity)
- Second output will take?
- (a) 90 mins; (b) 25 mins; (c) 50 mins

- Repetitively done processes
- End of the day, process has work in progress
- Automobiles; cabinets; checks; loan applications; invoices; airplanes

Activity Efficiency for a primed process

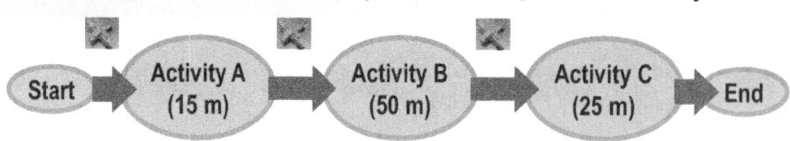

Start → Activity A (15 m) → Activity B (50 m) → Activity C (25 m) → End

- Now have available output at start of shift for all
- The first output will be available in 25 mins (time for the last activity)
- In the remaining (460 − 25) = 435 mins, we can get (435 / 50) = 8.7 units
- In a workday we get (1 + 8.7) = 9.7 units
- Note in this scenario, we started with a ready output in between activities or with a **primed process**

College of Engineering & Technology
EAST CAROLINA UNIVERSITY

Veneer Technologies, Inc.
Lean Six-Sigma Yellow Belt (LSSYB) Training

Example of Activity Efficiency

- Ideal expected output = 15.33 units
- Expected output (un-primed line) = 8.4 units
- Expected output (primed line) = 9.7 units
- Ideal expected output = 15.33 units which is 100% efficiency or ideal efficiency
- **Activity Efficiency (un-primed) = (Expected output for un-primed) / (Ideal expected output)**
- AE(U) = 8.4 / 15.33 = 0.548 = 54.8%
- **Activity Efficiency (primed) = (Expected output for primed) / (Ideal Expected Output)**
- AE(P) = 9.7 / 15.33 = 0.633 = 63.3%

	Expected Outputs	Activity Efficiency
Ideal	15.33	100.0%
Un-primed	8.4	54.8%
Primed	9.7	63.3%

So how do our numbers work out?

We don't even know how long it takes to make one product!

Need to Know Total Activity Time

Station #	Job Description	Reading 1	Reading 2	Best reading
WS-1	Main members			
WS-2	Wings			
WS-3	Tail section			
WS-4	Fuselage cabins			
WS-5	Landing gear			
WS-6	Cockpit			
WS-7	Ailerons			
WS-8	Jet engines			
WS-9	Fuel tanks			
WS-10	Rudder			
WS-11	Inspection			

(Activity Time columns) — **ACTUAL TIMES**

College of Engineering & Technology
EAST CAROLINA UNIVERSITY

Veneer Technologies, Inc.
Lean Six-Sigma Yellow Belt (LSSYB) Training

Min/Max Cycle Times

- Takt time = 14.4 secs
- Total activity time = _____ secs
- Total workstations = _____

- What is the minimum & maximum cycle times that we can have?

- Minimum C/T = _____
- Maximum C/T = _____

Deciding the best C/T for the process

Station #	Job Description	Activity Time	# FTE	Total C/T	Slack
WS-1	Main members				
WS-2	Wings				
WS-3	Tail section				
WS-4	Fuselage cabins				
WS-5	Landing gear				
WS-6	Cockpit				
WS-7	Ailerons				
WS-8	Jet engines				
WS-9	Fuel tanks				
WS-10	Rudder				
WS-11	Inspection				
		Totals			
		Planned C/T			

College of Engineering & Technology
EAST CAROLINA UNIVERSITY

Design of Round 2 Layout

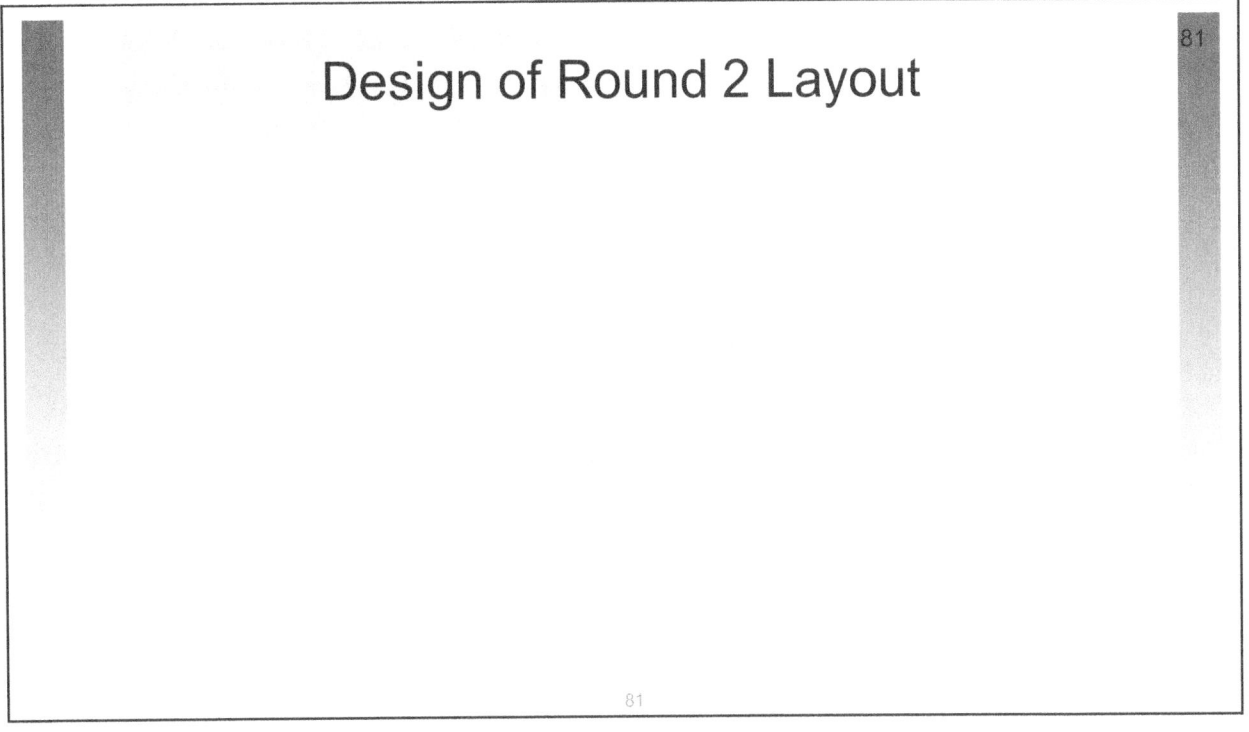

Expected Output (Un-primed)

- All activities will be done in C/T = _____
- First output will be done in = _____
- Every output after that will take = _____

- Expected output after 1st part
-   = (Shift time – first part time) / (C/T)
-   = [(6 mins x 60) – ____)] / (____)
-   = [360 – ____] / (____) = ____ outputs

- Expected output (un-primed) = 1 + ____ = ____ outputs

Veneer Technologies, Inc.
Lean Six-Sigma Yellow Belt (LSSYB) Training

Expected Output (Primed)

- All activities will be done in C/T = _____
- First output will be done in = _____
- Every output after that will take = _____

- Expected output after 1st part
- = (Shift time − first part time) / (C/T)
- = [(6 mins × 60) − ____)] / (____)
- = [360 − ____] / (____) = _____ outputs

- Expected output (primed) = 1 + _____ = _____ outputs

Ideal Expected Output

- Process capacity or total people-seconds in process = (shift time) × (number of people)
  - = (6 min × 60) × (_____)
  - = 360 × ____ = _____ secs

- Activity time per plane = ____ secs

- Ideal Expected Output
  - = Output if all time is used productively
  - = (Total people-seconds) / (Activity time per plane)
  - = (_____ secs) / (_____ secs) = _____ outputs

College of Engineering & Technology
EAST CAROLINA UNIVERSITY

Expected Activity Efficiency

- Ideal expected output = _____ units
- Expected output (un-primed line) = _____ units
- Expected output (primed line) = _____ units
- Ideal expected output = _____ units = 100% efficiency or ideal efficiency

- **Activity Efficiency (un-primed) = (Expected output for un-primed) / (Ideal expected output)**
- AE(U) = _____ / _____ = _____ = _____ %

- **Activity Efficiency (primed) = (Expected output for primed) / (Ideal Expected Output)**
- AE(P) = _____ / _____ = _____ = _____ %

Summary of Process Design

	Expected Outputs	Activity Efficiency
Ideal		100.0%
Un-primed		
Primed		

- We can now compare these numbers to the actual efficiency numbers!
- Let us run the improved process in unprimed and prime state
    - No material handlers
    - Inspector doubles as the shipping agent. Can fix obvious problems in outputs
    - Use Kanbans to control overproduction

Veneer Technologies, Inc.
Lean Six-Sigma Yellow Belt (LSSYB) Training

Actual Round 2 Results

Station #	Station	Unprimed Inventory	Unprimed Rejects	Primed Inventory	Primed Rejects
	Good airplanes				
	Lead time for 1st plane				

Metrics for Round 2

Process Metrics	Round 2
Time to make one airplane	
Airplanes made	
Total inventory in process	
Airplanes rejected	
Number of people	
Productivity: airplanes / # people	

Let us calculate the efficiency numbers

College of Engineering & Technology
EAST CAROLINA UNIVERSITY

Veneer Technologies, Inc.
Lean Six-Sigma Yellow Belt (LSSYB) Training

Calculating Activity Efficiency

- Actual output (un-primed): _____
- Actual efficiency (un-primed)
- = (Actual output) / (Ideal expected output)
- = _____ / _____ = _____ = _____%

- Actual output (primed): _____
- Actual efficiency (primed)
- = (Actual output) / (Ideal expected output)
- = _____ / _____ = _____ = _____%

Calculating Activity & Operating Efficiency

	Ideal expected units	
Unprimed	Expected output units	
	Expected AE	
	Actual AE	
Primed	Expected output units	
	Expected AE	
	Actual AE	

- Operating Efficiency(U) = (Actual AEU) / (Expected AEU)
- = _____ / _____ = _____ = _____%
- Operating Efficiency(P) = (Actual AEP) / (Expected AEP)
- = _____ / _____ = _____ = _____%

College of Engineering & Technology
EAST CAROLINA UNIVERSITY

Veneer Technologies, Inc.
Lean Six-Sigma Yellow Belt (LSSYB) Training

Further Analysis

	Round 1	Round 2 (Primed)
Time to make first airplane		
Airplanes made		
Total inventory in process		
Airplanes rejected		
Number of people in cell		
Productivity: airplanes / # people		

Improvement (Round 2 over Round 1)

	Ratio	Up/down	Percent
Time to make first airplane			
Airplanes made			
Total inventory in process			
Airplanes rejected			
Number of people in cell			
Productivity: airplanes / # people			

Improvement = [(New number – Old number) / (Old number)] x 100

Negative = down   Positive = up

Cycle Times – Primed Process

Output #	Cycle Time	Output #	Cycle Time	Output #	Cycle Time	Output #	Cycle Time
1		11		21		31	
2		12		22		32	
3		13		23		33	
4		14		24		34	
5		15		25		35	
6		16		26		36	
7		17		27		37	
8		18		28		38	
9		19		29		39	
10		20		30		40	

Mean Cycle Time	#DIV/0!
SD of Cycle Time	#DIV/0!

Calculate mean cycle time and standard deviation (SD) of cycle times!

College of Engineering & Technology
EAST CAROLINA UNIVERSITY

Veneer Technologies, Inc.
Lean Six-Sigma Yellow Belt (LSSYB) Training

Create Histogram of C/Ts

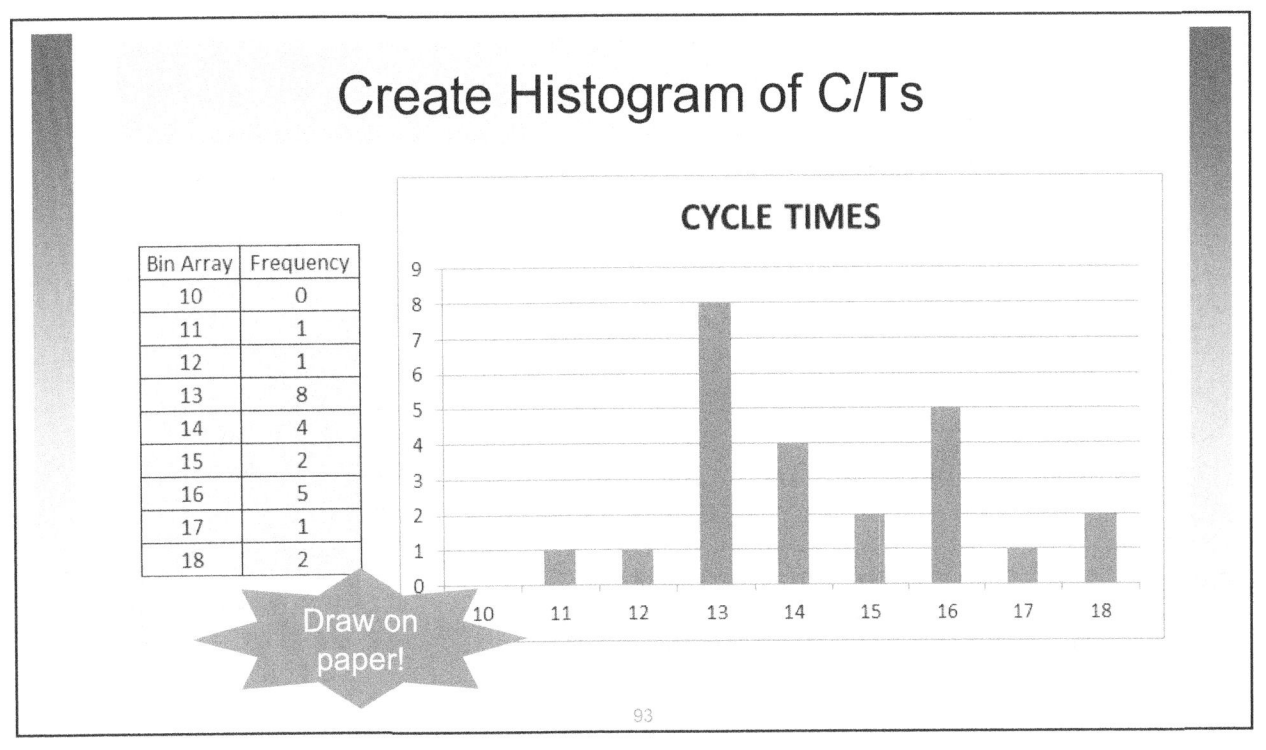

Bin Array	Frequency
10	0
11	1
12	1
13	8
14	4
15	2
16	5
17	1
18	2

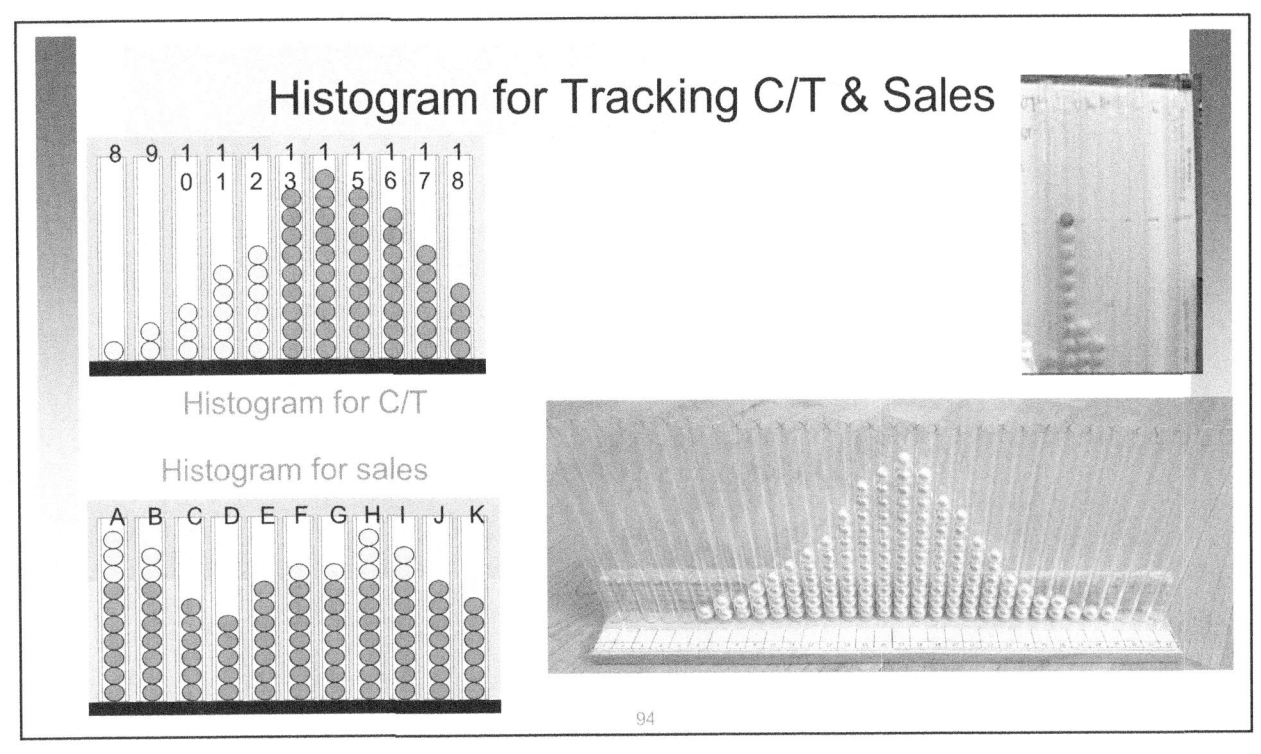

CYCLE TIMES

Draw on paper!

Histogram for Tracking C/T & Sales

Histogram for C/T

Histogram for sales

A B C D E F G H I J K

College of Engineering & Technology
EAST CAROLINA UNIVERSITY

Veneer Technologies, Inc.
Lean Six-Sigma Yellow Belt (LSSYB) Training

Create Histogram

Draw here!

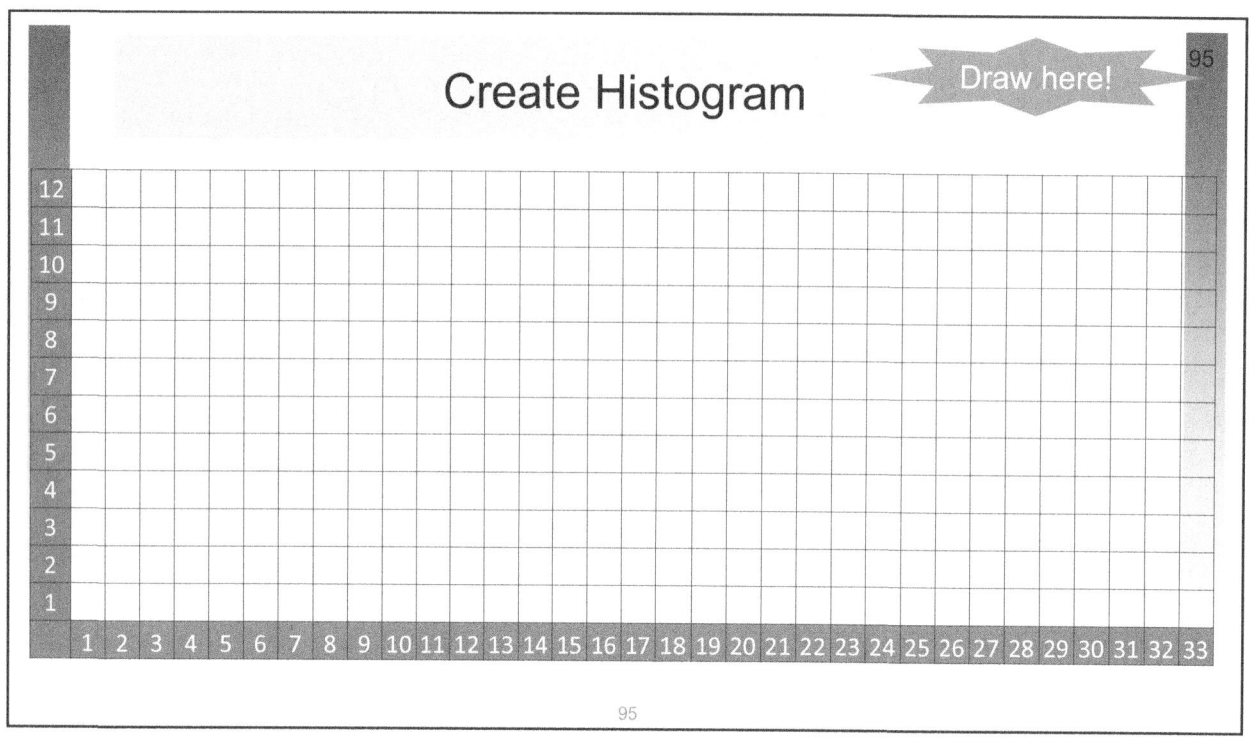

3C Store Fixtures Inc., Wilson, NC

- Industrial Engineer
- January 2010
- Building results with Legos®

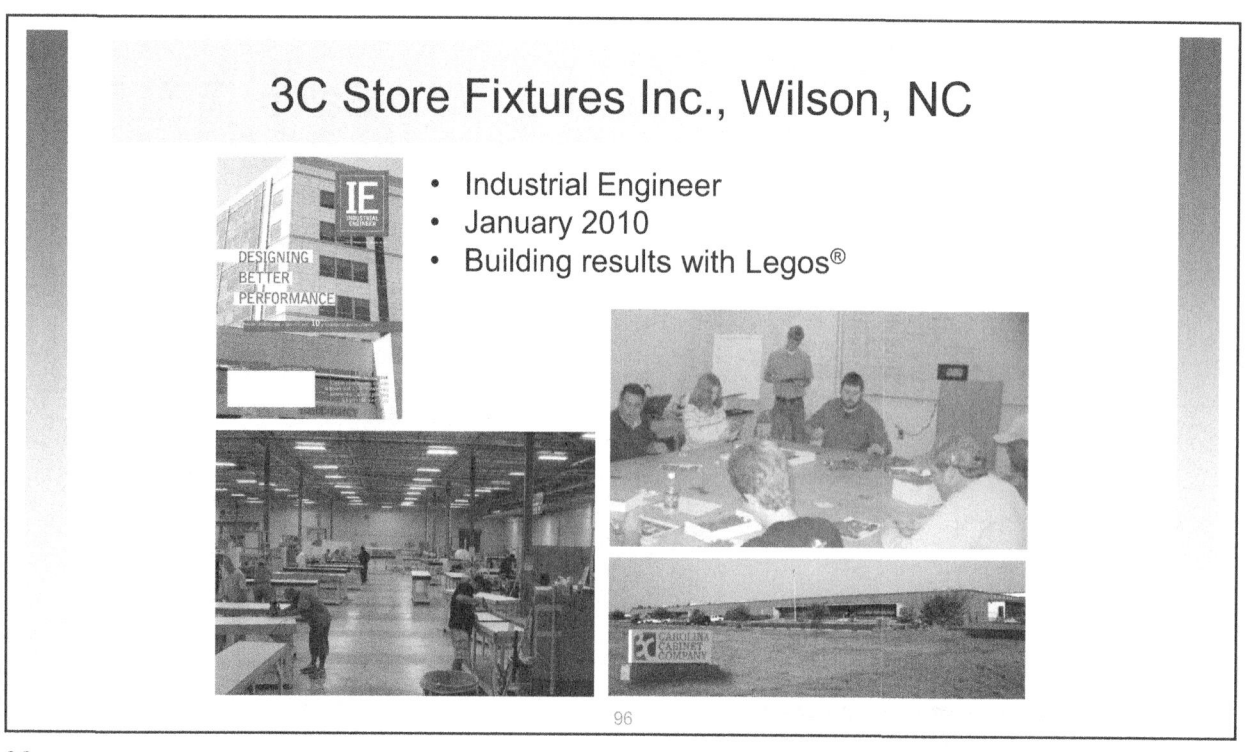

College of Engineering & Technology
EAST CAROLINA UNIVERSITY

3C Store Fixtures Inc., Wilson, NC

- Order for 1,200 "home accessory fixtures" for J. C. Penney
- 1st week (comments from industrial engineer):
  - "Operators organize work area based on experience"
  - "Assembly team has always been motivated"
  - "They were all helping each other do their best, but workloads and cycle times were very unbalanced"
- 1st week results:
  - Produced 53 units working as hard as they could
  - Delivery estimate 1,200 / 53 = 22.6 weeks

Simulation and Kaizen Training

- 2nd week:
  - Cells restructured and balanced using worker input
  - A floater/spider provided
  - Clock in work area for cycle time and Takt time
  - Produced 120 units per week
- Delivery estimate:
  - 11.6 weeks: Week 1: 53; Week 2: training; Another 9.6 weeks [(1200 – 53) / 120]
  - Finished order in 11.6 weeks instead of 22.6
  - Improvement = (11.6 - 22.6) / 22.6 = -0.49
  - Delivery time went down by 49%

College of Engineering & Technology
EAST CAROLINA UNIVERSITY

Veneer Technologies, Inc.
Lean Six-Sigma Yellow Belt (LSSYB) Training

Previous and Current State

PREVIOUS STATE

#	Station	People	Cycle Time	Operation Time	Effective O/T
1	Assemble top and bottom	2	40	80	96
2	Assemble sides	1	48	48	48
3	Laminate glue application	1	20	20	48
4	Part glue application	1	18	18	48
5	Laminate application & trimming	4	15	60	192
6	Cleaning	2	12	24	96
7	Caster assembly	2	15	30	96
8	Packaging	2	20	40	96
	TOTALS	15		320	720
	CYCLE TIME FOR LINE		48		

CURRENT STATE

#	Station	People	Cycle Time	Operation Time	Planned O/T
1	Assemble top and bottom	4	18	72	72
2	Laminate glue application	1	16	16	18
3	Laminate application & trimming	1	15	15	18
4	Trimming and filling	2	18	36	36
5	Cleaning	1	10	10	18
6	Caster assembly	1	15	15	18
7	Packaging	2	15	30	36
	TOTALS	12		194	216
	CYCLE TIME FOR LINE		18		

Improvement Metrics

Row #	Description	Formula	Previous State	Current State
A	Total Operation time		320	194
B	Planned total operation time		720	216
C	Observed cycle time (minutes)		48	18
D	Actual # of employees		15	12
E	Calculated capacity (people mins)		6900	5520
F	Calculated ideal expected output	+E/A	21.56	28.45
G	Actual time for first part (mins)	+A	320	194
H	Calculated unprimed output	+(460-A)/C	2.92	14.78
I	Calculated unprimed AE	+H/F	13.5%	51.9%
J	Calculated primed output	+460/C	9.58	25.56
K	Calculated primed AE	+J/F	44.4%	89.8%
L	Calculated unprimed output per week	+5 x H	14.58	73.89
M	Calculated primed output per week	+5 x J	47.92	127.78
N	Calculated unprimed units/employee/week	+L/D	0.97	6.16
O	Calculated primed units/employee/week	+M/D	3.19	10.65
P	Primed Actual Outputs per Week	Actual run	53	120
Q	Primed Actual AE	+[P/(5 x F)]	49.2%	84.3%

College of Engineering & Technology
EAST CAROLINA UNIVERSITY

Results and Savings Realized

- Operating efficiency (OE) = 94% of planned goals
  - OE = (Actual AE)/(Calculated AE) x 100
  - OE (primed process) = 84.3% / 89.8% = 0.94 x 100 = 94%
- Lead time:
  - Reduced from 22.6 weeks to 11.6 weeks
  - Lead time reduced by 49% (included training & initial time)
- FTE: Reduced from 15 to 13 (12 + 1 floater)
- Eliminated: Overtime, second shift and extra training
- Total tangible savings:
  - 15 people for 12.6 weeks @ $18.00 per hour (including benefits) + 2 people for 9 weeks @ $18.00 per hour
  - 15 x 12.6 x 18 x 40 + 2 x 9 x 18 x 40 = $136,080 + $12,960 = $149,040 (includes floater)

Lessons: Employees and Management

- Lessons learned by employees:
  - The only way to keep efficiency high is to work as a team
  - Have constant product flow from the first station to the last
  - Any glitch in one of the activities is a loss in time for the entire process
  - Loss time can never be recouped
  - Get preventive maintenance done within the process cycle

- Lessons learned by management:
  - Involve the entire workforce
  - Convince workforce of potential for productivity improvement
  - Set levels for efficiency metrics in consultation with employees
  - Provide means to constantly monitor how well employees are doing
  - Make it into a game with rules and rewards! Create a motivated and empowered workforce

Veneer Technologies, Inc.
Lean Six-Sigma Yellow Belt (LSSYB) Training

Role of Quality in Lean Six-Sigma

- Each activity has a customer. Customer decides output quality!
- All responsible for output; move only good output to customer
- Customer coming back for more information is an "incomplete & inaccurate" output
- Use samples and standards to be clear on quality metrics
- Consider using self-checking means (Poka yoke) for quality
- Use % first pass yield (%FPY) or % complete and accurate (%C&A)
- Good source for downloading quality tools:
  - https://asq.org/quality-resources/quality-tools

First Pass Yield (FPY)

- How many good outputs result in the first pass at an activity station?
- FPY ratio = (# accepted / # handled)
- %FPY = {(# accepted / # handled)} x 100
- 45 good outputs result from processing 60 at an activity station

  - First Pass Yield (FPY) ratio
    = (# accepted / # handled)
    = 45 / 60 = 0.75

  - %First Pass Yield (%FPY)
    = 0.75 x 100
    = 75%

Note: This does not include any reprocessing or rework done on the rejected output!

An alternate name for %FPY is %C&A.

%C&A = percentage complete & accurate!

College of Engineering & Technology
EAST CAROLINA UNIVERSITY

Veneer Technologies, Inc.
Lean Six-Sigma Yellow Belt (LSSYB) Training

Rolled Throughput Yield (RTY)

- Yield for the entire process
- Say, there are 3 activities in a process; FPY ratios for the 3 activities are:
  - $FPY_1 = 0.90$, $FPY_2 = 0.94$, and $FPY_3 = 0.97$
  - Reject rates are 10%, 6% and 3%
- What is the RTY ratio and %RTY?

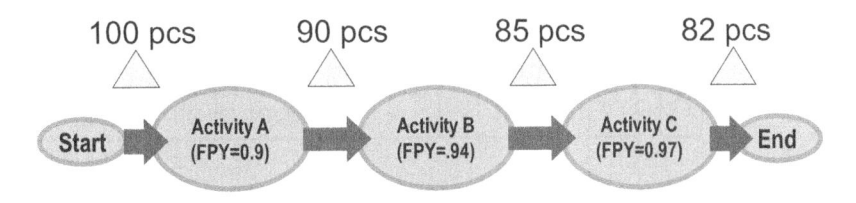

100 pcs → Start → Activity A (FPY=0.9) → 90 pcs → Activity B (FPY=.94) → 85 pcs → Activity C (FPY=0.97) → 82 pcs → End

- RTY ratio = (0.90 x 0.94 x 0.97) = 0.82 or %RTY = (0.82 x 100) = 82%

Examples of %RTY

- 1. What is the %RTY for a process with 3 activities that starts out with 1,200 products. The %FPY for the first activity is 89%, the second activity produces 992 outputs and the reject rate for the third activity is 5%.

Start → Activity A → Activity B → Activity C → End

- 2. What would be the %RTY for a process with 10 activities that each have a reject rate of 5%?

What is Our %RTY?

College of Engineering & Technology
EAST CAROLINA UNIVERSITY

Veneer Technologies, Inc.
Lean Six-Sigma Yellow Belt (LSSYB) Training

Calculating %RTY for Round 1

Station #	Inventory Created	# of Rejects
WS-1		
WS-2		
WS-3		
WS-4		
WS-5		
WS-6		
WS-7		
WS-8		
WS-9		
WS-10		
WS-11		
Totals		

Activity Stations: 1, 2, 3, 4, 5, 6, 7, 8, 9, 10, 11

A	Completed	
B	Inventory	
C	Unsatisfactory	
D	Processed	
E	Satisfactory	
F	FPY (Ratio)	
G	RTY (Ratio)	Product of all FPY's

- Round 1: %RTY = _____ %
- Where rejects happen, matter!

Calculating %RTY for Round 2 (primed)

Station #	Inventory Created	# of Rejects
WS-1		
WS-2		
WS-3		
WS-4		
WS-5		
WS-6		
WS-7		
WS-8		
WS-9		
WS-10		
WS-11		
Totals		

Activity Stations

A	Completed	
B	Inventory	
C	Unsatisfactory	
D	Processed	
E	Satisfactory	
F	FPY (Ratio)	
G	RTY (Ratio)	Product of all FPY's

- Round 2: %RTY = _____ %

College of Engineering & Technology
EAST CAROLINA UNIVERSITY

RTY Improvement from Round 1 to 2

- %RTY for Round 1 = _____%
- %RTY for Round 2 = _____%
- Improvement = [(New number–Old number)/(Old number)] x 100
- %RTY improvement =
  - [(%RTY for Round 2 - %RTY for Round 1) / (%RTY for Round 1)] x 100
- %RTY improvement =

- %RTY also called simply "yield" or "process yield"

Pointers on Brainstorming

- Right mix of people assembled—GIGO
- Participants given time to think
- Initially, no discussion allowed
- Participants build on each other's ideas
- No idea is too crazy!
- Develop exhaustive list of ideas
  - Go around the room asking individually for input
- Refine list and categorize
  - Seek clarification for suggestions
  - Mutually exclusive, collectively exhaustive (MECE)

Veneer Technologies, Inc.
Lean Six-Sigma Yellow Belt (LSSYB) Training

5-Why analysis & 7 Basic Quality Tools

1. Cause-and-effect diagram
2. Check sheets
3. Control charts
4. Histograms
5. Pareto chart
6. Scatter diagrams
7. Stratification charts

	Why	Because	Details/Conclusions:
1	Why do employees have to search for tools?	The people who use them do not place them back in their places.	
2	Why do people who use the tools do not return them back to their places?	There has been a lot of retooling lately and people assume that they will need them soon anyway.	
3	Why do employees make the assumption that they will need the tools anyway, and that it is not worth returning them back to their places?	It is not clear what all specific tools will be needed for a particular setup, and the tool board on which the tools hang is near the supervisor's office.	Make a list of all tools that are needed for a specific setup.
4	Why are the tools not close to where the setup is done?	Everyone keeps losing the common tools and the supervisor decided it is best to keep tools close to her.	
5	Why do employees keep losing tools?	They do not have personal ownership of the tools.	Issue employees a set of tools that they can keep in a locked toolbox on wheels along with a list of tools needed for specific setups.

Simple yet effective!

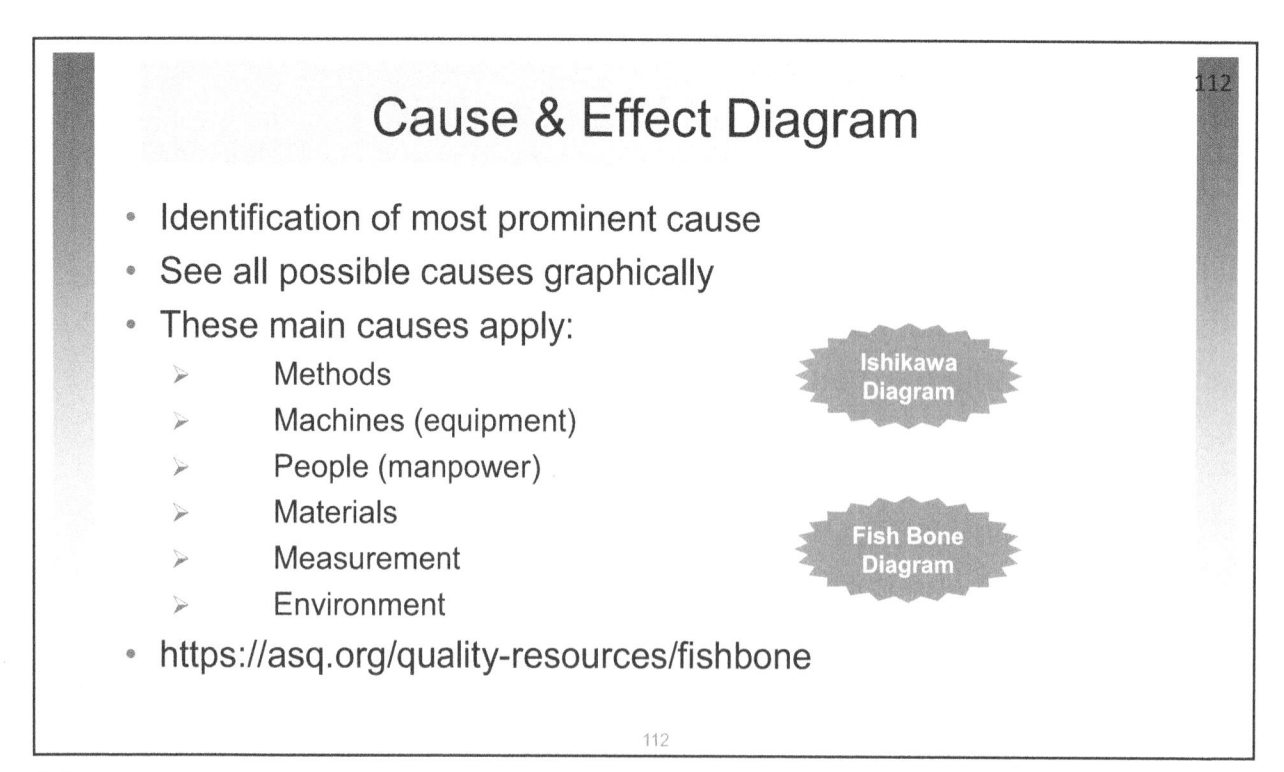

Cause & Effect Diagram

- Identification of most prominent cause
- See all possible causes graphically
- These main causes apply:
  - Methods
  - Machines (equipment)
  - People (manpower)
  - Materials
  - Measurement
  - Environment
- https://asq.org/quality-resources/fishbone

Ishikawa Diagram

Fish Bone Diagram

College of Engineering & Technology
EAST CAROLINA UNIVERSITY

Veneer Technologies, Inc.
Lean Six-Sigma Yellow Belt (LSSYB) Training

Cause & Effect Diagram

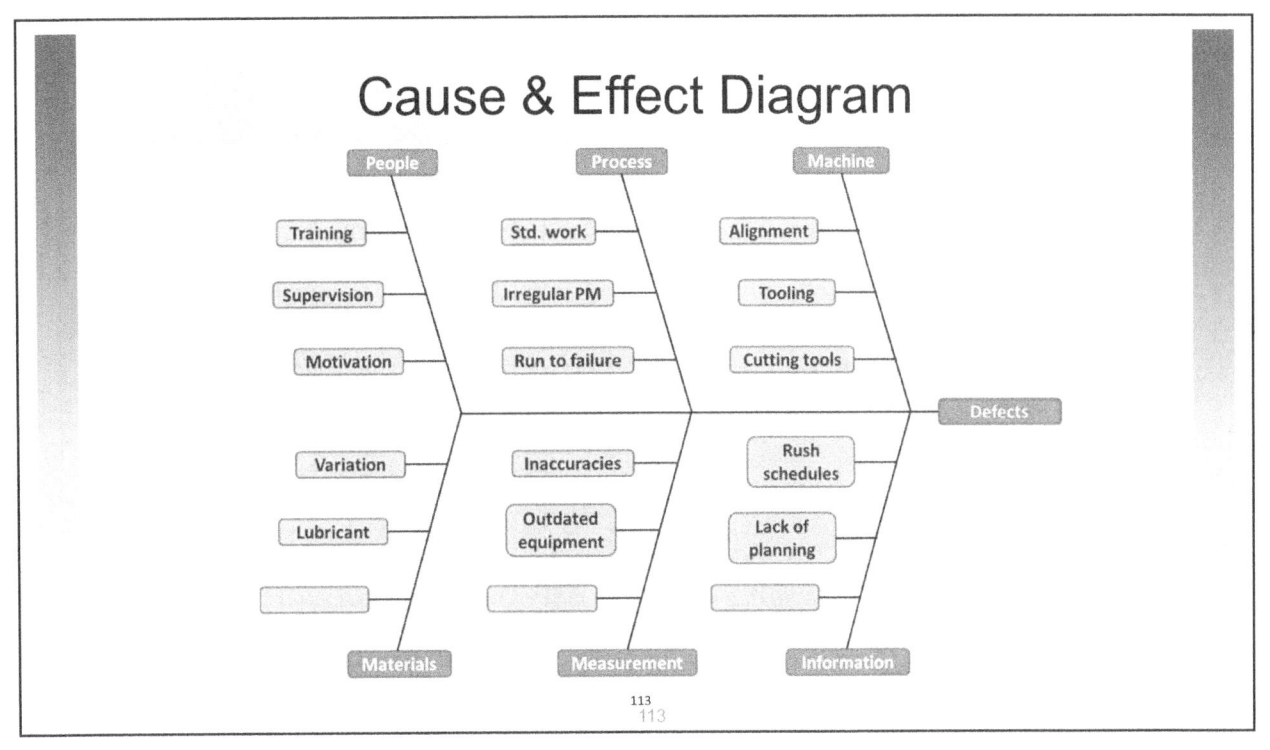

People:
- Training
- Supervision
- Motivation

Process:
- Std. work
- Irregular PM
- Run to failure

Machine:
- Alignment
- Tooling
- Cutting tools

→ Defects

Materials:
- Variation
- Lubricant

Measurement:
- Inaccuracies
- Outdated equipment

Information:
- Rush schedules
- Lack of planning

Fishbone Diagram With Solutions

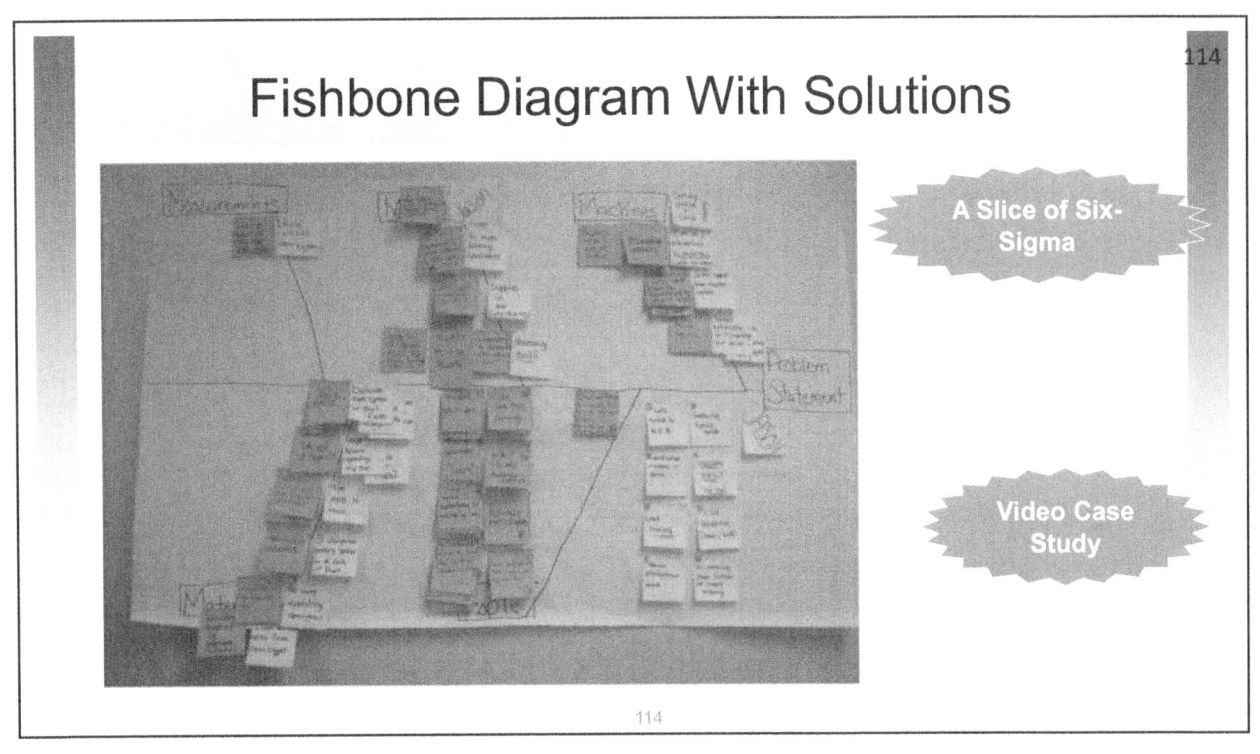

- A Slice of Six-Sigma
- Video Case Study

College of Engineering & Technology
EAST CAROLINA UNIVERSITY

Veneer Technologies, Inc.
Lean Six-Sigma Yellow Belt (LSSYB) Training

Check Sheets

- To collect basic real time data
- Make checkmarks
- To identify patterns
- Collect data in real time
- Quantitative or qualitative

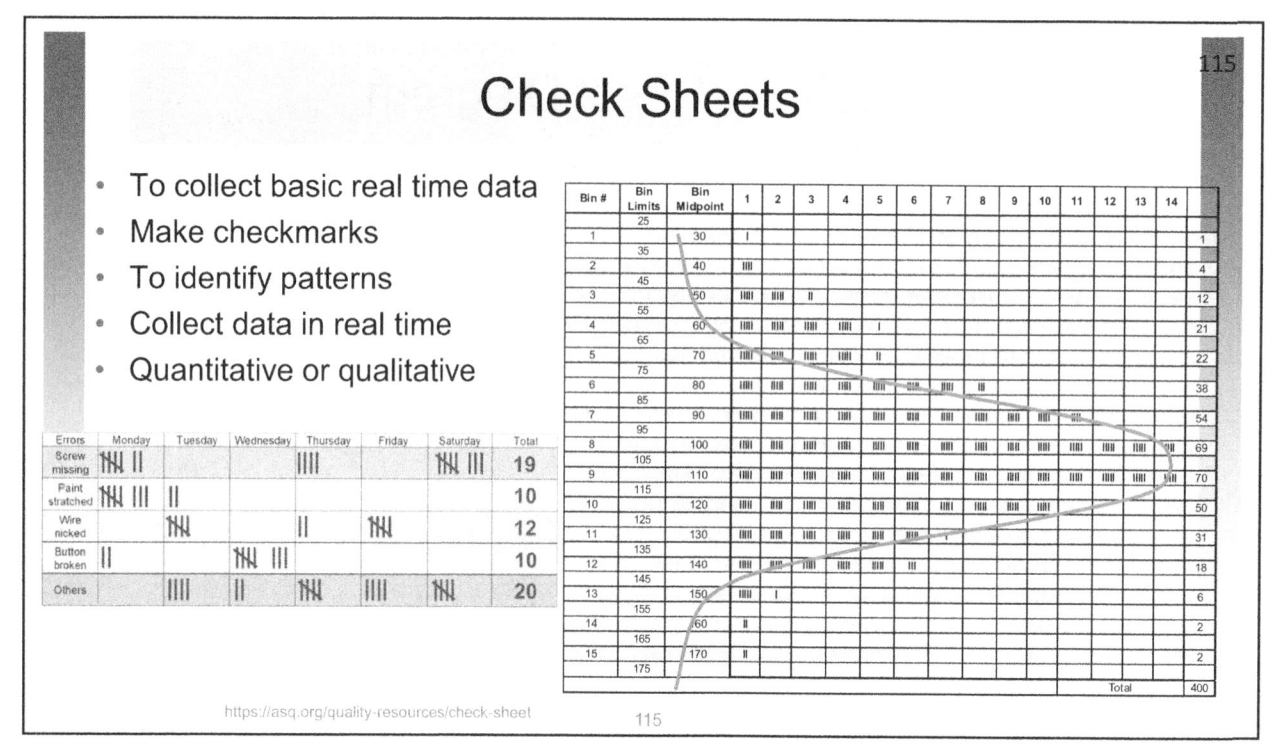

https://asq.org/quality-resources/check-sheet

Pareto Charts

- Special histograms or column graphs; Used to prioritize problems or opportunities
- Few problems present the most opportunity for improvement
- Identifies the "vital few" to allow us to ignore the "trivial many"
- 20% of problems present 80% opportunity for improvement
- Write idea on Post-It Notes or in Excel
- No critiquing of ideas; no bad idea; more the better; build on each other's ideas
- Create a list of ideas to vote on; apply MECE – mutually exclusive, collectively exhaustive
- Each person chooses 4 ideas; highest has a score of 4; Lowest has a score of 1
- Vote without influence from others
- Create percentages and cumulative %
- Create Pareto chart

The 80-20 Rule!

College of Engineering & Technology
EAST CAROLINA UNIVERSITY

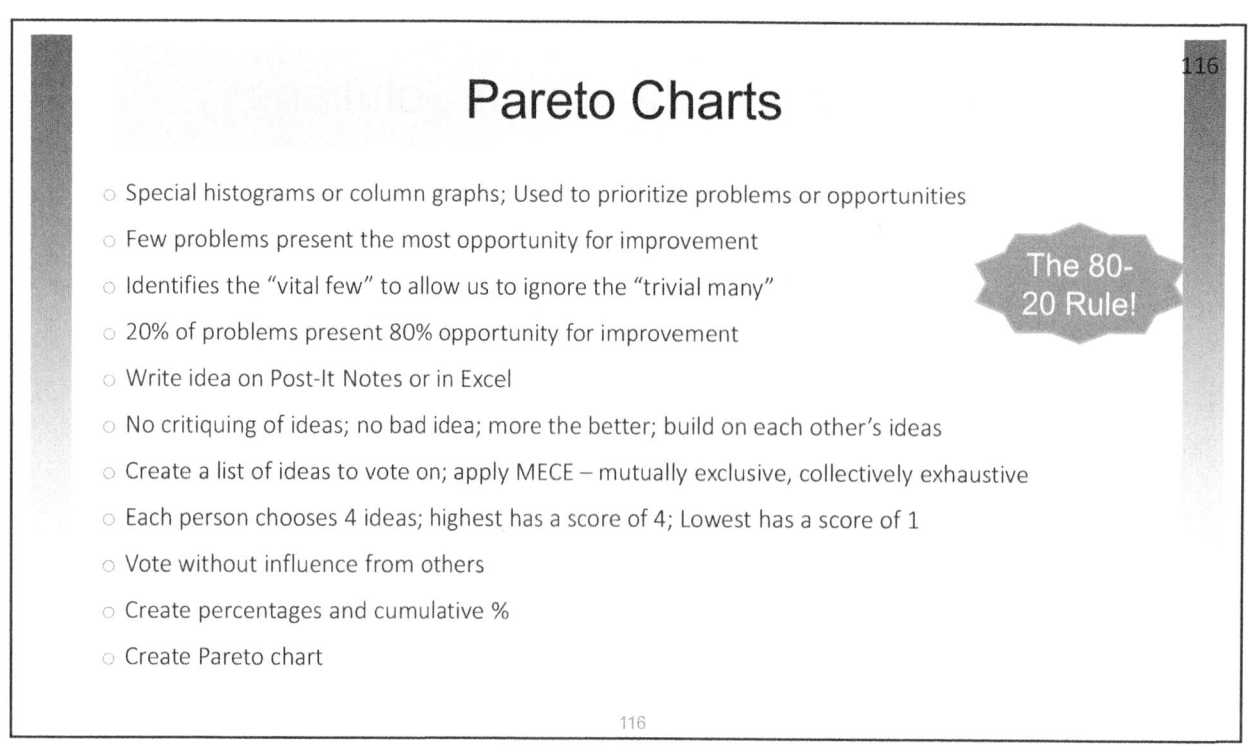

Veneer Technologies, Inc.
Lean Six-Sigma Yellow Belt (LSSYB) Training

Why do students at ECU not graduate in 4 years?

	Reasons for not graduating on time	S1	S2	S3	S4	S5	S6	S7	S8	S9	S10	S11	S12	S13	S14	S15	S16	S17	S18	S19	S20	S21	S22	S23	TOTAL
A	Legal issues																								0
B	Changing a major	4	4	4	4	4		3	4	4	4	4	3	4	4	1		3	4	1	4	3		4	70
C	Working instead of school			3							2	2	2			2									11
D	Did not show/failing class		1	3				1	1	3	3			3		4		4		4	2			1	30
E	Financial issues		2		1	3	2	2			3	1	2	3		4	2	2					2		29
F	Classes not being offered					3			1							3		1		3					11
G	Personal/mental problems	3		2				3		1						2	1		2		2			3	19
H	Physical injury				2				2																4
I	Partying and distractions	2	3		2	1	4		2		1				2	3	1		3	3					27
J	Transferring into university	1				1															1	4			7
K	Winning a lottery																						4		4
L	Pursuing other careers		1										1										1		3
M	Cursed by the cupola															1							3		4
N	Natural disasters																					1	2		3
O	Political issues																								0
P	Program shut down																								0
Q	Losing interest							4					4												8
		10	10	10	10	10	10	10	10	10	10	10	10	10	10	10	10	10	10	10	10	10	10	10	230

Plot Histogram

- Show individual percentages for each category

Reasons for Students Not Graduating in 4 Years

Category	Percentage
B	30.43%
D	13.04%
E	12.61%
I	11.74%
G	8.26%
C	4.78%
F	4.78%
Q	3.48%
J	3.04%
Other	7.83%

College of Engineering & Technology
EAST CAROLINA UNIVERSITY

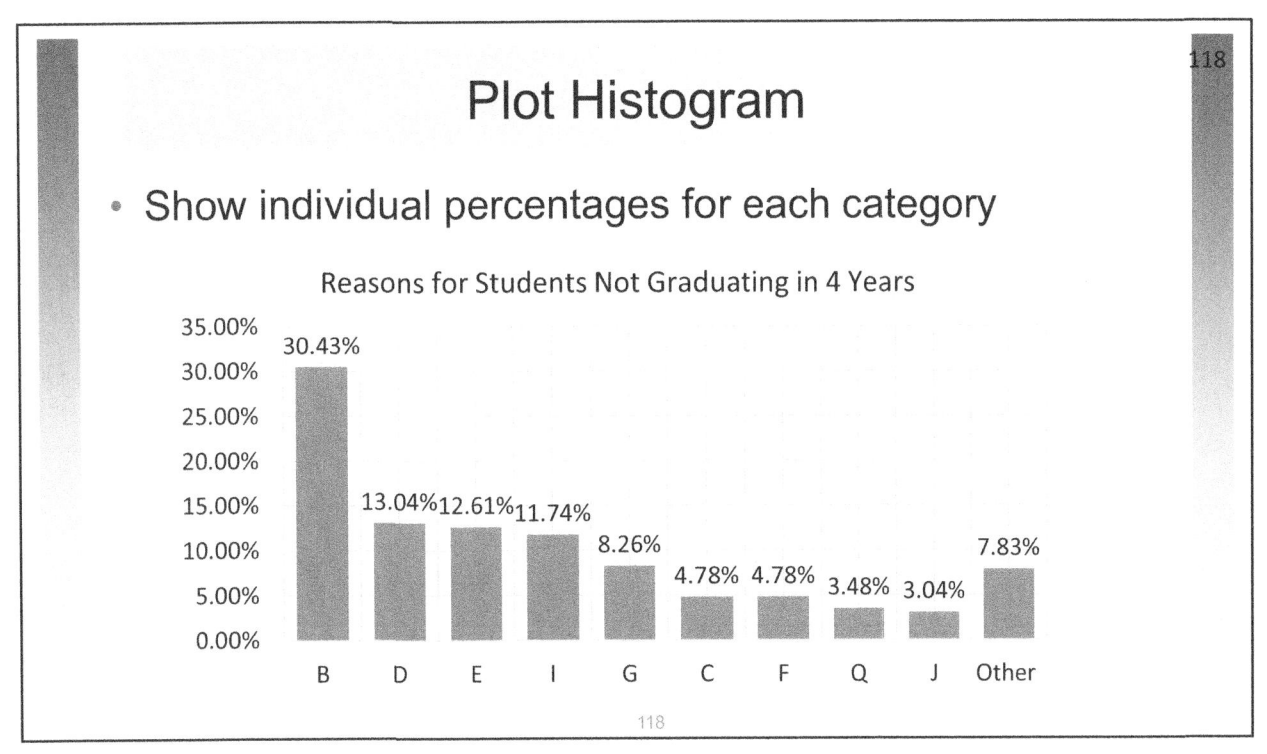

Veneer Technologies, Inc.
Lean Six-Sigma Yellow Belt (LSSYB) Training

Waterfall Pareto Chart

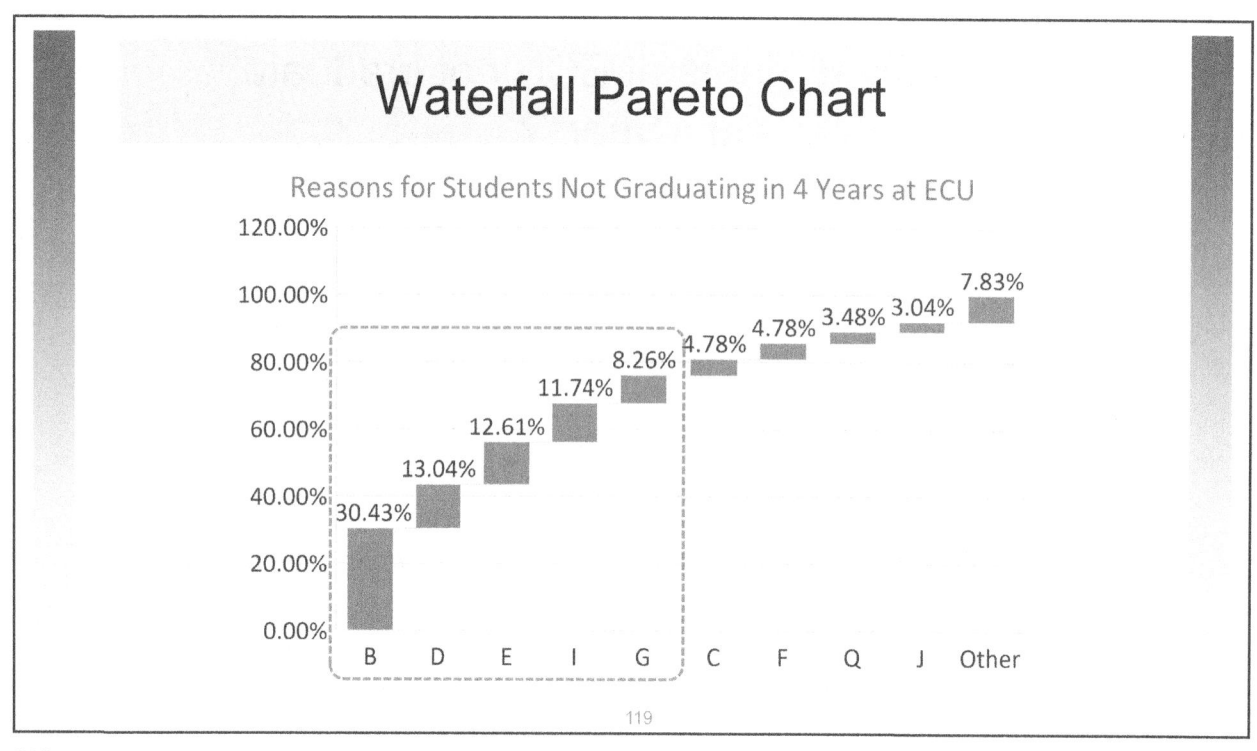

Reasons for Students Not Graduating in 4 Years at ECU

Category	Percentage
B	30.43%
D	13.04%
E	12.61%
I	11.74%
G	8.26%
C	4.78%
F	4.78%
Q	3.48%
J	3.04%
Other	7.83%

Control Charts

- Process stable, in control with 30 outputs
- Calculate mean, LCL, UCL from data
  - LCL = (mean − 3 x SD)
  - UCL = (mean + 3 x SD)
- Determine appropriate time interval
- Use chart to monitor process
- If point is out of control limits, investigate and correct
- Points should be randomly spread
- Are there trends created?
  - Is external influence playing on process?
  - Identify and eliminate
  - Central line to denote average for data

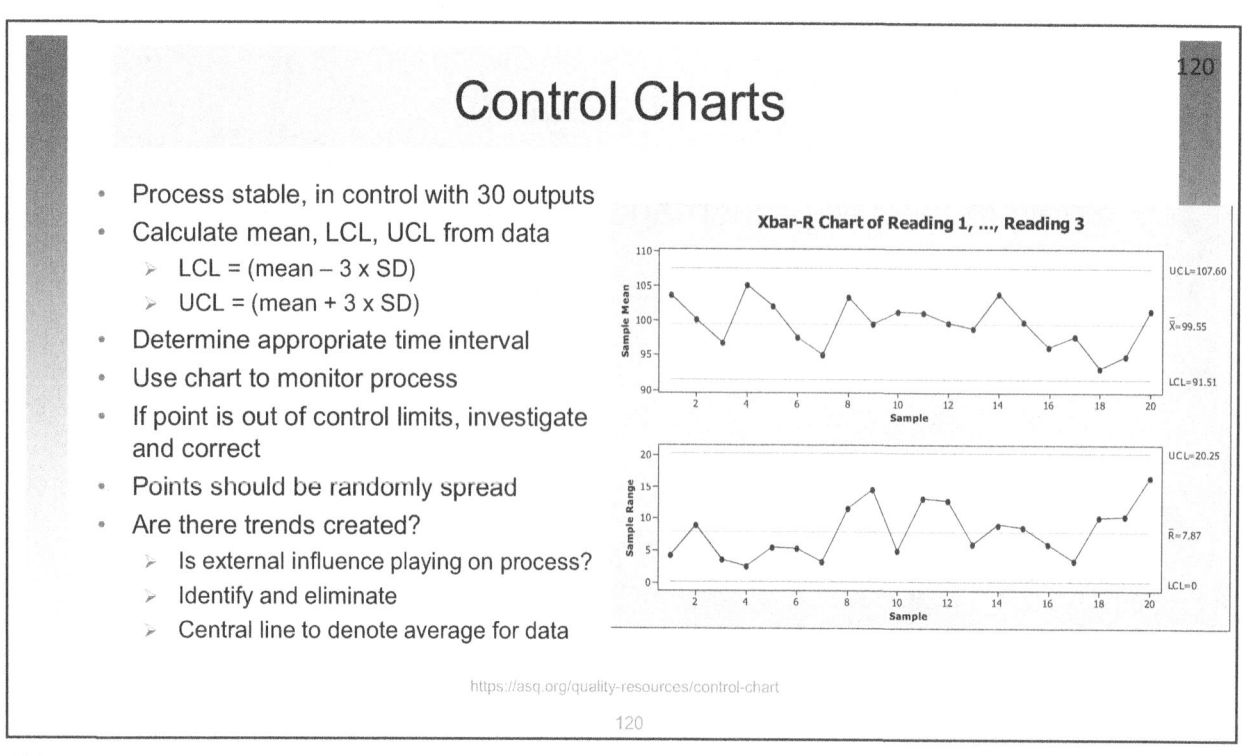

Xbar-R Chart of Reading 1, ..., Reading 3

UCL=107.60, $\bar{X}$=99.55, LCL=91.51
UCL=20.25, $\bar{R}$=7.87, LCL=0

https://asq.org/quality-resources/control-chart

College of Engineering & Technology
EAST CAROLINA UNIVERSITY

Closing Thoughts

- Abraham Lincoln
  - Important principles may, and must, be inflexible.
  - He has a right to criticize, who has a heart to help.
- Michael Jordan
  - Talent wins games, but teamwork and intelligence wins championships."
- Peter Drucker
  - There is surely nothing quite so useless as doing with great efficiency what should not be done at all!
- Dr. Edwards Deming
  - It is not necessary to change; survival is not mandatory!
- Aristotle
  - We are what we repeatedly do; excellence, then, is not an act but a habit!

https://blog.vantagecircle.com/management-quotes/

References

- MANUFACTURING INSIGHTS: Building a Lean Culture DVD; Copyright © 2006; Available from the Society of Manufacturing Engineers (SME); Product ID: DV06PUB15
- Womack. J. P. (2007). The Machine That Changed the World, Paperback (New edition). Simon & Schuster Ltd.
- George, M. (2003). Lean Six Sigma for Service : How to Use Lean Speed and Six Sigma Quality to Improve Services and Transactions (1st ed.). McGraw-Hill Education.
- Liker, J. (2020). The Toyota Way, Second Edition: 14 Management Principles from the World's Greatest Manufacturer (2nd ed.). McGraw-Hill Education.
- Ford, H. S. C. (2021). My Life and Work by Henry Ford in Collaboration with Samuel Crowther (First Edition). Garden City.
- Womack, J. P., & Jones, D. T. (2003). Lean Thinking: Banish Waste and Create Wealth in Your Corporation, Revised and Updated (2nd ed.). Free Press.
- Floyd, R. C. (2010). Liquid Lean: Developing Lean Culture in the Process Industries (1st ed.). Productivity Press.
- https://www.ted.com/talks/christine_porath_why_being_respectful_to_your_coworkers_is_good_for_business?language=en
- http://www.stuartlevine.com/wp-content/uploads/2010/12/Investors-Business-Daily.pdf

Made in the USA
Middletown, DE
26 May 2024